ALLEN, ATWOOD

Outta My Mind, Into His Heart

60 Devotions for Those with Mental Illness and Their Advocates

Karen Allen
Sharon Atwood

ISBN-13: 978-1-962168-20-5

"Sharon Atwood and Karen Allen have written a beautiful book of 60 devotions to support, inspire, and encourage those who struggle with mental illness. Each devotion comes from their hearts. Readers can participate in this journey as the authors have included simple and direct questions to answer, as well as space to record their answers, feelings, and opinions. I am impressed with this book written for both people with mental illness as well as those who love them."

— Denise George, author, co-administrator of Christian Writers for Life

"Karen and Sharon pull back the curtain and provide a personal look at the intersection of deep faith and friendship. They are transparent and vulnerable, sharing the joys and struggles of both those with mental illness and their advocates. Their message provides needed encouragement and real hope, promoting the kind of resiliency that honors Christ and displays the beauty of His Bride."

— Dr. Chris Jones, Senior Pastor, Meadow Brook Baptist Church

"You both reminded me how blessed I am to be my son's advocate and the source of all my needs in this difficult journey. So many emotions are swimming in my heart and mind. Jesus is my comforter and my strength! Thank you both for reminding me of that."

— Phyllis Stinson, mother of
adult son with schizophrenia

"Sharon and Karen discuss their personal and relational experiences with an open and honest simplicity that is both profound and relatable as they share the struggles, challenges and lessons of living with the realities of mental illness. They beautifully portray walking beside each other on their journey, each learning from the other and becoming better from their friendship. Their devotions inspire hope both for those who live with mental illness and those who strive to befriend, understand and support them."

— Lenora J. Enix, Psy.D.,
Clinical Psychologist

"Dealing with my brother's mental illness since I was 22 (that is 52 years), I was excited to read Karen and Sharon's book. Seeing the situation from Karen's viewpoint was familiar, but reading from Sharon's viewpoint made me stand up and listen. The two sides really make it come together."

— Barbara Harika, sister of sibling with a mental illness

"If I had to describe *Outta My Mind, Into His Heart* in one word, it would be honoring. It is honoring to people who deal with mental illness; it is honoring to people who come alongside loved ones dealing with mental illness; it is honoring to the Lord and His power and wisdom and healing; it is honoring to a beautiful friendship that has spanned decades. I am so grateful for this thoughtful devotional, and for the women who were anointed by God to write it."

— Mari Beth Poor, pastor and life coach

"Highly readable amazing collection of clinical and spiritual insights that contain healing for all of us. Thanks for your time, effort, and willingness to be vulnerable."

— Susan R. Sallin, CPPS,
President of NAMI
Birmingham, Alabama

Acknowledgments

A devotional book like this takes courage, prayer, and help from others whose talents extend beyond our own. The co-authors wish to thank the following for their expertise and willingness to guide us in completing this book:

To Karen's husband, George "Parky" Allen – Thank you for lending us your organizational skills and computer know-how to shape and finalize our manuscript.

To Denise George – Your encouragement and guidance were instrumental in spurring us on to do more than we thought was possible. We appreciate your mentorship throughout the process and beyond.

To Rebecca Pounds George – Your soothing words brought calm assurance. Thank you for leading us down worthwhile paths.

To Caroline Chamberlain – First, thank you for your friendship and continued support. You have been a prayer warrior for us throughout our publication process. Second, your artistic touch is a welcome addition to our book.

To Sandi Herron – Your love for God is displayed through your writing and beautiful art. Thank you for the serenity your artwork brings to induce relaxation and peace.

To Laura Klinner Brown – Your investment of time and talent into editing our book is much appreciated, helping to enhance the clarity, transition, and parallelism.

OUTTA MY MIND, INTO HIS HEART

We dedicate this devotional book to all those struggling with mental health issues and to their advocates.

THE BACKSTORY

Prayer changes things and sometimes that "thing" is us! God opens our eyes to give us new perspectives leading to unexpected outcomes.

One particular prayer did that for me. Sharon visited my church on a Sunday night and asked me to pray for her after the service. I agreed but with some hesitancy. I could see there was something different about her, but I didn't feel comfortable denying her a simple prayer.

Little did we know that God would answer that prayer, and many others, in ways we could never have imagined. That night Sharon asked if I would be willing to serve as her discipleship teacher. God answered her prayer when I said "yes." But God would also answer my prayer for a close friend with whom I could share spiritual conversations. Who would have ever believed a mentally ill individual from a broken background would become good friends with a Type A individual fifteen years her senior? I knew little about mental illness, and she knew little about non-chaotic living.

Fast forward twenty years. We have learned extensively from each other – me, about mental illness and what it takes to be a friend and mentor; and her, about managing life in an orderly fashion and accepting unconditional love. Our history could fill the pages of a book. So that's what we decided to do!

Karen Allen

INTRODUCTION

Millions of people in the United States, approximately one in five, are affected by the symptoms of mental illness every day of their lives. Only half receive treatment. Perhaps part of the reason is that society has stigmatized individuals with mental illness.

Mental illness is the leading cause of disability in the U.S. It encompasses a wide range of conditions that affect mood, thinking, feeling, and behavior causing significant distress or impairment in daily living. Types of mental illness vary from anxiety, eating, mood, personality, developmental, and substance abuse to psychotic disorders. Since we know good health is important, why are we close-minded when it comes to good mental health?

We wrote these devotions because we are tired of hiding behind the stigma and want to throw a lifeline to the mental health community and its advocates. Caregivers and advocates deserve the recognition of presence as well as those dealing with mental illness because they are impacted by the illness, too.

We begin each section with a devotion focusing on a personal scenario and a biblical reference associated with that scenario. Our devotions are transparent and sometimes intense as we address issues often glossed over. *Every scenario is real.* We have lived through them or continue to. Sharon shares from her perspective as a person with bipolar disorder complicated by other past diagnoses. Then Karen shares the next day from her perspective as an advocate on the same or a similar topic. Therefore, the devotions are written as a pair totaling 60 devotions incorporating 30 topics. Each devotion identifies the writer with her name under the devotion's title.

Following each set of devotions, a section called **The Heart of the Matter** asks three thought-provoking questions for you to answer according to your circumstances. Next, the **What's On Your Heart?** section provides an opportunity for you to record your thoughts and feelings.

Our prayer is that this devotional book offers hope and encouragement amid difficult circumstances encountered with mental health issues. We are not mental health professionals and are not offering a treatment plan for any illness. We do not address every type of mental illness or mental health issue, but we feel our topics are relevant and offer insight into a godly and healthier perspective. God cares, understands, and is present even in the midst of mania, anxiety, and depression. The goal is to look beyond ourselves and our circumstances to embrace God's compassionate and loving heart. In other words, although we may be out of our minds, we can cling to His heart.

"Encourage the exhausted, and strengthen the feeble. Say to those with anxious heart, 'Take courage, fear not.'" (Isaiah 35:3-4 NIV)

WHAT A FRIEND

By Sharon

*Friends come and friends go, but a true
friend sticks by you like family.*
Proverbs 18:24 MSG

Dealing with mental health issues can put a lot of pressure on friends. That's why some of my friends have quietly disappeared, while others have hung in there, enduring the bad times. When mania consumes me, my anxiety level rises above the already higher-than-normal level of most people. I am jittery, illogical, and in need of comfort. Disorganization and spontaneity create relational conflicts. Reaching out for help, I sometimes turn to the rationality of remaining friends who have opened their homes as a respite or who have helped me gather my belongings before going to the hospital. Conversely, when I am depressed, I have friends with whom I can share a meal or play a board game.

Scripture shows many examples of relationships between friends. For example, Jonathan and David were best friends who encountered difficult times but stuck by each other's side until death. Paul was a friend and mentor to Barnabas, teaching him righteous living and steadfast faith. I am thankful to have friends like Jonathan and Paul.

God is faithful to send friends who provide

encouragement and comfort in times of need. Without special friends, I believe my bouts of depression and anxiety would be more pronounced. Supportive friends often demonstrate the love found in a friendship with the love of Jesus. Their love can be all-encompassing to cover any sorrows or disappointments.

Friends come and go. Some are meant to be in our lives for only a season, but those who remain by our side for a lifetime are indeed a blessing. Family members have no choice, but friends who are like family choose to be part of your life – good or bad.

Prayer: Lord, let us be thankful for true friends.

OUTCASTS WELCOMED

By Karen

A vast crowd brought to him people who were lame, blind, crippled, those who couldn't speak, and many others. They laid them before Jesus, and he healed them all.
Matthew 15:30 NLT

Mental illness. Those two words can bring out unusual responses in people. Some become visibly uncomfortable; others disengage from the conversation; however, some are sympathetic, offering personal experiences or encounters and occasionally taking advantage to mention a loved one. I wonder if society will always have a stand-offish attitude, either consciously or unconsciously, towards those in the mental health community.

The Bible mentions a strange encounter in I Samuel 21. David feigns insanity in front of a king out of fear about what he might do to him. David acts unruly by scratching on doors and drooling down his beard. The king dismisses David, questioning why his officials would bring another madman into his midst to be his guest.

Too often, this is the image society has of someone with a mental illness. But that is not typical. Still, society has stigmatized the mental health community with an unwarranted blanket of shame and blame. Why? Primarily because they are fearful and/or uneducated. As an advocate, friends, and coworkers have advised me more than once to dissolve my relationship with Sharon.

The New Testament gospels tell about the life of one who chose to associate with those who were stigmatized by society. He frequently conversed with lepers, beggars, widows, prostitutes, sex offenders, the disabled, the blind, the deformed, those with unclean diseases, the demon-possessed, and soothsayers. He brought hope. He brought healing. He brought forgiveness. His love reached out. His heart had compassion, and his touch brought restoration. His name? Jesus. Do you know this one named Jesus? He knows and cares about you.

Prayer: Jesus, show me Your love and compassion today.

Treat people as if they were what they ought to be and you help them become what they are capable of being.[1]

~ Johann Wolfgang von Goethe, German poet ~

Heart of the Matter

1. Who are some of your friends who stick beside you through thick and thin?

2. What challenges does mental illness present that impact friendships?

3. Do you feel you have been stigmatized in some way because of your mental illness or by your association with someone who has a mental illness? If so, how?

Words from His Heart

Two people are better off than one, for they can help each other succeed.

Ecclesiastes 4:9 NLT

What's On Your Heart?

TEACH ME TO BE WISE

By Sharon

*Listen to counsel and receive instruction so
that you may be wise later in life.
Proverbs 19:20 HCSB*

The stained-glass windows beckoned me to enter the church sanctuary. After the evening service, I approached a lady in the congregation to request that she pray with me. After praying together, I asked if she would be willing to disciple me. Her answer was yes. In the coming weeks, we met and discussed Bible lessons and their application. Like Paul giving wise counsel to Timothy, she imparted wisdom to me.

When my mother became terminally ill with brain cancer, she asked my mentor and discipleship teacher to watch over me. Eventually, I came to recognize her as my godmother, or more specifically, a Godmother whom God had sent to me in my time of need. My godmother offered wise counsel, not just spiritually but practically.

We should be receptive to those who have experienced more of life so that we may benefit from their wisdom. Value and worth can be gained. My godmother's wisdom helped me walk a little taller and built my self-esteem.

Paul was a mentor to Timothy, referring to him as "my own son in the faith" (I Timothy 1:2). Paul taught him to preach the Good News and live a godly life. In a good mentoring relationship, the mentor and the mentee learn treasured insights and viewpoints from one another. Having an older mentor could not only add stability to our lives, but it could offer growth, comfort, encouragement, and hope.

Today I still listen to my godmother's counsel. Her words have influenced me to live a more godly life and to open my heart to being a mentor for others.

Prayer: Lord, help us learn wisdom for spiritual growth and practical living from those around us.

DIFFERENT STROKES

By Karen

*What good is it, dear brothers and sisters, if
you say you have faith but don't show it by your
actions? Can that kind of faith save anyone?*
James 2:14 NLT

Mentor, second Mom, friend, discipleship teacher,
caregiver, guardian, advocate, godmother – these are
some of the titles I have been called regarding my
relationship with Sharon. Crazy, challenging, honorable,
loyal, and strange are some of the descriptions
surrounding that relationship. The truth is we don't fully
understand our relationship! All we know is that God
brought us together. Just like Pharaoh's daughter took a
sentimental liking to a three-month-old crying baby boy
floating in a basket on the river, I felt compassion for a
25-year-old woman who was visiting my church and
asked for prayer.

Twenty years and countless episodes later, it is clear
that God knew what He was doing. He used the most
unlikely person to draw me unto Himself to show me
more about His character.

Circumstances, status, education, or lifestyle offer
no parameters to God's plans. He can use us, each one of
us. The question is, are we willing? Are we obedient to
serve in ways that are unknown or uncomfortable to us?

God often uses the ordinary to do the extraordinary. You don't have to look far when you see the brood of disciples Jesus picked. Peter, an ordinary fisherman, became the rock upon which Jesus said He would build His church; but he first had to be obedient and follow.

I may not be a biological mother to Sharon; neither was Pharaoh's daughter to Moses. But I have become a Godmother responding to a call that has opened my eyes to a population of sometimes misunderstood, overlooked, dismissed, or stigmatized individuals whom God loves no less than anyone else. The role of a mental health advocate must surely bring a smile to God's face.

Prayer: Father, help me love those who are different from me. Let my faith be seen in my actions.

If you are successful, it is because somewhere, sometime, someone gave you a life or an idea that started you in the right direction. Remember also that you are indebted to life until you help some less fortunate person, just as you were helped.[2]

~ Melinda Gates, former wife of Bill Gates ~

Heart of the Matter

1. Do you have a mentor? If so, who? If not, whom would you like to be your mentor?

2. What characteristics and/or qualifications do you look for in a mentor?

3. Compare and contrast between being a mentor and a friend.

Words from His Heart

Give instruction to a wise man, and he will be yet wiser: teach a just man, and he will increase in learning.

Proverbs 9:9 KJV

What's On Your Heart?

FINDING A NEW PEACE

By Sharon

*Peace I leave with you; my peace I give you.
I do not give to you as the world gives. Do
not let your hearts be troubled and do not
be afraid.*
John 14:27 NIV

I sat on the edge of my bed, afraid, with my head in my hands. The shadows played off the walls in my room. Anxiety gripped my chest in anticipation of unanswered questions. After all, this was a psychiatric ward. I didn't know what to expect since this was the first time I'd ever been in a place like this. The nurses were friendly, but the loud and angry patients made me nervous.

Questions swirled around in my head. *What would the doctor say? Would he prescribe new medicine? How long would I have to be here? When would someone come to visit me?*

The answers to my questions slowly came. The doctor changed my medicine, which meant my body had to readjust. How many days I would remain in the hospital was unknown and dependent upon the response to the medication changes. Visitation days were empty and tearful, with no visitors.

Despite my worry and fear, every morning, as I awoke, the Lord placed a song of praise upon my lips. I enlisted other patients to sing along. My outlook began to improve slowly. Somehow, even in the midst of my anxiety, I rediscovered peace. I found the same peace in the scripture passage – a peace not of this world. Although I could not deny my fear, I have found that peace can overcome fear when my heart is troubled, but I must call upon the Peacemaker. Comfort is available in His prevailing peace.

Do you have that peace in your life?

Prayer: When we face our fears, O Lord, let us embrace Your triumphant peace.

STRENGTH TO OVERCOME

By Karen

He gives power to the weak and strength
to the powerless.
Isaiah 40:29 NLT

I felt like I had been gut-punched. Sure, it was an overreaction, but it was how I felt. Sharon called to say she had been admitted to the hospital and wanted me to visit her in the psychiatric unit. How could I do that? I had never been to a psychiatric unit before. Strange people roamed those halls. Besides, I was still dealing with the fact that she was there at all! I had tried my best to prevent her from taking that step to be hospitalized as she had done in the past, but she felt otherwise.

My heart raced as we spoke on the phone. *What do you mean, 'here's my password'?* Do I have to use a password to call the hospital? This was way out of my comfort zone. After hanging up, I cried. Hard. How was I going to support my friend when I couldn't even face a visit to the psychiatric ward?

My sheltered upbringing rendered me faint of heart and weak of spirit. I needed to focus less on me and more on Him. That was the only way to press through my emotions. "Weak" and "powerless" was a good description of my mental state. "Power" and "strength" was the remedy. I prayed not only for Sharon but also that I could find the strength to be a source of encouragement and stability despite my frailty. God not only cared about Sharon's state of mind, but He cared about mine as well. I needed that reminder for this hospitalization and others to follow.

God meets us where we are every time. He gives power and strength when we call upon His name.

Prayer: Dear Lord, give us strength in the moments when we feel the weakest.

It isn't enough to talk about peace. One must believe in it. And it isn't enough to believe in it. One must work at it.[3]

~ Eleanor Roosevelt ~

Heart of the Matter

1. Identify a time when you felt anxious.

2. What did you do to regain your peace?

3. When has God given you strength during a moment of weakness?

Words from His Heart

*For God is not the author of confusion,
but of peace, as in all churches of the
saints.*

I Corinthians 14:33 KJV

What's On Your Heart?

WISE COUNSEL

By Sharon

*But the Counselor, the Holy Spirit – the
Father will send Him in My name - will
teach you all things and remind you of
everything I have told you.*
John 14:26 HCSB

Professional counseling comes in different forms:
individual counseling, couples or marriage counseling,
family counseling, and group counseling. All forms
involve building relationships to meet worthwhile goals.
Listening, observing, reflecting, and empathizing are
usual components during a counseling session.
Counselors learn things by asking questions, but,
according to the passage, the Holy Spirit teaches – He
does not ask questions. That's because the Holy Spirit
already knows the answers!

Different approaches are used by counselors to
address problems, develop life skills, and reveal the truth
to bring clarity. One counselor may focus on the past to
discuss childhood experiences, another may center on
immediate goals, and another may look at current
practices impacting future outcomes. My counselor says
she strives for peace with the past, joy in the present, and
hope for the future. That works for me!

The reasoning behind our behavior is important to a

counselor, but the morality of our behavior concerns the Holy Spirit. No matter how bad my actions were, are, or ever will be, I will never be condemned.

The focal passage today identifies the Holy Spirit as a Counselor. The Holy Spirit can use my past, present, and future to offer counsel at any time of the day or night. I like that the Holy Spirit has accessibility to my entire being at any given time. It gives me comfort, especially since my physical counselor is not always available.

I've had many counselors through the decades – some good, some not so good – but I wouldn't be without one. I believe God uses counselors to bring healing. My experience confirms it!

Prayer: Holy Spirit, counsel me in your ways.

BETTER WISE UP

By Karen

I will instruct you and teach you in the way
you should go; I will counsel you with my
loving eye on you.
Psalm 32:8 NIV

Some of the best advice I ever received was simple yet
profound. My husband and I were driving home one
evening when I confessed that I had difficulty grasping
everything cancer had brought into my life. He suggested
I focus on one day at a time and not look any further.
How freeing!

Why hadn't I thought of that? His advice gave me a
new perspective. My mind had been so clouded trying to
cope and maintain some kind of normalcy that I couldn't
see a logical solution. I needed wisdom from a
trustworthy source to guide me.

Counseling is often prescribed as a means of therapy
to help manage life more effectively. Intimate details and
feelings may be shared in a safe environment with
another unbiased person. By allowing someone to fill
that role, valuable advice and instruction can be
provided. We've often heard that stepping away from a
situation can help us see things more clearly.

It's no surprise that royalty and individuals in great

leadership positions often seek counsel. Even the President of the United States has many advisers. Why? Because, as the scripture says, wisdom may be gained through wise counsel to make better and more precise decisions.

Throughout the Bible, we see kings, prophets, priests, tribes, and nations seeking counsel. Although King David was a mighty warrior, he routinely consulted with advisers regarding battle strategies.

Trust in the counselor must exist in order for advice `to be accepted and implemented. David sought elders and apostles as counselors, but the one he most sought for counsel was God. This practice still stands true today.

Prayer: Father, may we earnestly seek counsel in Your Living Word so that we may grow in wisdom.

Strength and growth come only
through continuous effort and
struggle.[4]

~ Napolean Hill, self-help author~

Heart of the Matter

1. What characteristics do you think a counselor should have?

2. How do you see the Holy Spirit as a counselor?

3. Identify a time you have sought wise counsel from the Word.

Words from His Heart

Plans fail for lack of counsel, but with many advisers they succeed.

Proverbs 15:22 NIV

What's On Your Heart?

ONLY FOR TODAY

By Sharon

Therefore, do not worry about tomorrow,
for tomorrow will worry about itself. Each
day has enough trouble of its own.
Matthew 6:34 NIV

The "to-do" list for the week kept growing longer and longer in my head. My palms were sweaty, and my stomach was in knots as I ran my fingers through my hair. How was I ever going to get everything done on time? My stress level was rising like the heat of a hot summer day.

All I needed to do was approach each item one at a time, but the solution eluded me. I was so concerned about tomorrow's tasks that I could not focus on today's "to-do's."

While leading the Israelites into the Promised Land, Moses became overwhelmed with all the responsibilities he assumed– proof that even great leaders of the Bible can overextend themselves. He worked from morning until evening, serving as a judge to hear disputes. Day after day, he felt the pressure of settling cases between quarreling parties.

Exhaustion and constant demand from a vast number of people were noticed by Moses' father-in-law Jethro. "This is not good," he said, "What are you really accomplishing?" Jethro warned Moses that he would wear himself out (Exodus 18:13-27). He suggested a plan that involved delegating Moses' duties to qualified people, leaving Moses to hear and rule only on the major cases. Moses heeded his father-in-law's advice to manage his strained time.

Time management often involves breaking down long lists into shorter, more manageable parts. I could accomplish small tasks each day and complete my entire list for the week successfully while, at the same time, reducing my stress level. I simply needed to focus on today, not tomorrow.

Prayer: Lord, help me to seek Your guidance to take one day at a time to avoid becoming overwhelmed about tomorrow.

THE PERFECT STRESSBUSTER

By Karen

*You will keep in perfect peace all who trust
in you, all whose thoughts are fixed on you!*
Isaiah 26:3 NLT

A hot bath, playing the piano, a stroll through the neighborhood. I tried them all. My mouth was still dry, my shoulders ached, and sleeping was a challenge. Forgetfulness became an issue, too. As much as I wanted to deny it, I was in stress overload. I forced myself to compartmentalize as best I could, but thoughts still raced through my head.

Is this how Esther felt when she risked her life to ask the king to save her people from annihilation (Esther 7:3)? Could this be how Joseph responded when he learned that his fiancé Mary was pregnant and that he wasn't the father (Matthew 1:18-19)? How about the stress Hosea felt being married to a known prostitute who bore children from adulterous affairs (Hosea 1:2)?

In each of these situations, God is the common denominator. Esther, Joseph, and Hosea all trusted Him to find peace. God is the One who intervened for Esther to find favor with the king. Not only did she save her people, but she killed her nemesis with the same weapon he was going to use to kill her cousin.

God sent an angel to Joseph in a dream, telling him that Mary was visited by the Holy Spirit and was now carrying the Savior of the world. Joseph was not to "divorce" Mary as he planned but was to marry her and be the earthly father of Jesus.

Hosea obeyed God and showed his unfaithful wife, Gomer, relentless love and mercy to demonstrate how God does the same for us even when we stray.

With these bold examples, I wonder why I put myself in such a frenzied state. God can help me. God can and will help you, so let's tap into that perfect stressbuster.

Prayer: Lord, when my stress grows by the day, rein in my anxiety to focus and lean on You. I want the perfect peace You promise.

The reason why you're always stressed is because you want this moment to be something that it's not. You just stop and you accept this moment for what it is.[5]

~ Oprah Winfrey ~

Heart of the Matter

1. When you get overwhelmed with too much to do, how do you handle it?

2. What are some ways that you have found that work well for you in dealing with stress?

3. Do you think that God can handle your stress? Are you willing to let Him?

Words from His Heart

Have I not commanded you? Be strong and courageous! Do not be terrified nor dismayed, for the Lord your God is with you wherever you go.

Joshua 1:9 NASB

What's On Your Heart?

HE KNOWS MY NAME

By Sharon

As a father has compassion on his children,
so the Lord has compassion on those who
fear him.
Psalm 103:13 NIV

"Daddy, Daddy, will you please toss the softball around with me?" was a little girl's pleading that fell on deaf ears. Maybe it was my father's schizo-bipolar disorder characterized by extreme high and low moods accompanied by delusions. Perhaps it was his medications. His medication caused aloofness, withdrawal, and increased sleepiness. Nonetheless, he was not there for me as a father should be for his daughter.

Webster's dictionary defines the word *father* as "one who has begotten a child." But fatherhood includes more than just a begotten child. Fathers, like mothers, are pillars in developing a child's physical, spiritual, educational, social, and psychological well-being. Fathers are intended to be the head of the household. Therefore, children expect their fathers to establish and enforce the rules of the house. They also look to their fathers to provide physical and emotional security. My father did none of those things.

Unlike my earthly father, my Heavenly Father,

Abba Father, has a personal and intimate relationship with me. He knows the number of hairs on my head (Luke 12:7); He knows what I am going to say (Psalm 139:4); He knows my every thought (Psalm 94:11) and He knows my name (Exodus 33:17). Numerous examples are found in the Bible of God or an angel of God calling out the names of His children: Samuel (I Samuel 3:4), Moses (Exodus 3:4), Mary (Luke 1:30), and Saul (Acts 9:4).

No matter what type of earthly father we have, we can praise God that we have a compassionate Heavenly Father... even though He may not play ball!

Prayer: Help me know You more as my Abba Father as You know me.

HONOR AT ALL TIMES

By Karen

Honor your father and mother, as the Lord
your God commanded you. Then you will live
a long, full life in the land the Lord your God
is giving you.
Deuteronomy 5:16 NLT

The Bible is clear that we are to honor our parents. In fact, it is one of the Ten Commandments given by God to Moses in the Old Testament, the same Ten Commandments we live by today. Honoring one's parents is not difficult when you are from a Christian home with loving parents. While I may not have always agreed with my parents, I respected them and obeyed their decisions, knowing they had my best interests at heart.

But what about a Dad who introduces pornography to his daughter? Do you still honor him? What about a mother who overlooks a child's sexual abuse going on under her roof? Do you still honor her? The complicated answer is "yes." "How can that be?" you ask. Because the commandment is not contingent upon actions – immoral as they may be. The commandment addresses the child's role.

I better understood the duty and depth of this commandment through Sharon's circumstances. She demonstrated honor to her parents despite growing up in a dysfunctional environment. I sometimes found myself angry about that honor, feeling as if it were undeserved. We must remember that forgiveness is not a prerequisite for showing honor.

For example, a story in Genesis 9 is seen with Noah and his three sons. After drinking too much wine, Noah went into his tent. Upon finding his father drunk and naked, one son dishonored his father, leaving him to go tell his brothers. The other two brothers took a robe and respectfully backed into the tent to cover their father's nakedness without looking. Showing a lack of responsibility and honor, one son was cursed; the other two were blessed. Guess which ones?

No matter the circumstances, God expects a child to honor their parents at all times. Sharon did just that.

Prayer: God, help me honor my parents at all times regardless of how I feel.

Forgiveness is not an occasional act;
it is a constant attitude.[6]

~ Dr. Martin Luther King, Jr. ~

Heart of the Matter

1. What kind of relationship did you have with your parents during your childhood?

2. How do you relate to God as your Abba Father?

3. What are some ways that you honor your parents?

Words from His Heart

Listen, my son, to your father's instruction, and do not ignore your mother's teaching.

Proverbs 1:8 NASB

What's On Your Heart?

ANXIETY CURE

By Sharon

Search me, God, and know my heart;
test me and know my anxious thoughts.
Psalms 139:23 NIV

My palms were sweaty as my heart beat rapidly. My chest felt as though an elephant was sitting on it. A feeling of impending doom hovered, and my thoughts raced like a horse approaching the finish line. I was having a panic attack.

Anxiety can be characterized by nervousness, restlessness, hyperventilation, sweating, and blocked concentration. Anxiety is often associated with fear of the unknown. These anxious feelings should remind us to place our trust in God, who holds the future.

Numerous characters in the Bible were no strangers to anxiety. Gideon was a military hero, judge, and prophet. One would think a man of such notoriety would not have anxiety issues, but he did. He was so insecure that he requested signs from the Lord not once but three times! God provided Gideon and three hundred soldiers with a ram's horn and clay torch. Gideon and his soldiers encircled the camp and defeated the horde of Midianites with noise and lights (Judges 6-7). Gideon relinquished his anxiety to place his trust in God. Victory was the result.

Jacob is another example. He stole his brother Esau's birthright and his father's blessing. Jacob knew Esau held a grudge and wanted to kill him, so he fled. Years later, the brothers met again. In great fear and distress, Jacob prepared an animal offering for Esau and divided his camp as a means of escape. But Esau ran to his brother with an embrace and kiss. All was forgiven (Genesis 33).

Like Gideon and Jacob, God knows our anxious thoughts and can turn them into positive results. We must capture those thoughts and surrender them into the hands of God, remembering He holds the future.

Prayer: Lord, calm my anxious heart when it becomes restless and full of worry. Help me lean upon You and trust Your guidance.

WHY ME?

By Karen

Don't worry about anything; instead, pray
about everything. Tell God what you need,
and thank him for all he has done.
Philippians 4:6 NLT

Ah, my favorite "go-to" verse whenever anxiety starts to creep in. Not worrying about anything covers a lot of ground. And there's a whole lot of "ground" when it comes to being a mental health advocate and caregiver. Feeling overwhelmed at times comes to mind. How can I juggle work, my marriage, my family, household demands, and church and still be available to deal with mental health crises? What if I do something wrong? Why was I chosen to be a mental health advocate anyway? I don't always know the right thing to do.

Moses had questions, too, when he was chosen to lead the Israelites out of Egypt. Who am I to appear before Pharaoh? Who am I to lead the Israelites out of Egypt? What if they won't believe me or listen to me? I cannot speak well. Send anyone else (Exodus 3-4).

Just as the Lord gave Moses the capacity to endure hardship after hardship, the Lord gave me the tenacity to withstand manic episodes, depressive bouts, hospitalizations, disappearances, and unwarranted outbursts. Did I handle each event successfully? No. Did Moses handle each event successfully? No. But the same God that was with Moses is with me. He is available to anyone who calls out to Him.

I try to follow the guidelines of the scripture passage above. I pray about everything. I tell God what I need. I try not to worry (though that is still a work in progress). But when the situation is over, I always thank Him for what He did.

Prayer: Even though I will always have questions, help me not to worry and to lift my cares to You in prayer.

Maintaining a godly perspective is one of
the most powerful ways to acknowledge
that God is greater than our
circumstances.[7]

~ Karen Allen, co-author of *Outta
My Mind, Into His Heart* ~

Heart of the Matter

1. What are some techniques you can use to practice capturing your anxious thoughts?

2. List some things that cause you anxiety.

3. Develop a plan to help conquer your fear the next time it pops up. Write it here so that you may refer to it.

Words from His Heart

*When anxiety was great within me,
your consolation brought me joy.*

Psalm 94:19 NIV

What's On Your Heart?

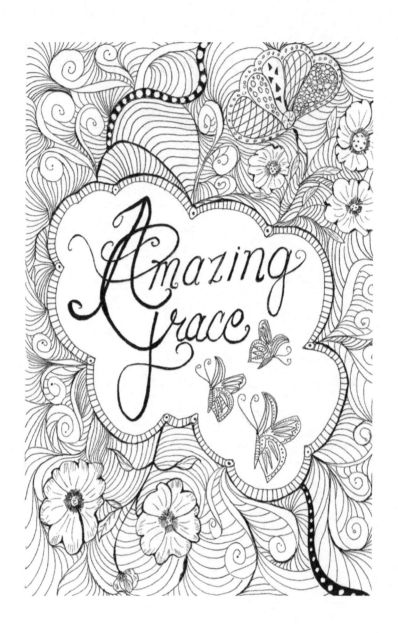

WHY SO BLUE?

By Sharon

Do not grieve, for the joy of the Lord
is your strength.
Nehemiah 8:10b NIV

I was irritable and utterly hopeless, not having slept well for days. Food did not appeal to me since I had no appetite. No doubt about it, I was depressed. Hours turned into days, days into weeks. A dark tunnel closed in around me. Searching for a way out, I tried reading but couldn't concentrate long enough to make sense of the words. I turned on the television, but it was just noise, not a source of pleasure. Nothing seemed to lighten my mood. However, experience had taught me that my depression would subside with time, but the waiting in between was long and hard.

Several characters in the Bible are recorded as having faced depression at some point in their lives, including David, Jeremiah, Hagar, Rachel, and Jacob. We find Elijah fleeing into the wilderness from King Ahab and Queen Jezebel in I Kings 19. He sat down under a tree and fell asleep, but when he awoke, he prayed that he might die.

"I've had enough; take my life."

Amid his depression, angels brought him bread and water, providing strength for Elijah to travel on and fulfill the Lord's commands.

Knowing that people have overcome depression since the days before Christ not only gives us relieving company but should also bring us comfort. Nehemiah shows us that grief can be overcome with joy.

The focal passage reminds us that joy in the Lord is our strength. Joy is not the same as happiness; joy is a deep, inner feeling. The joy of the Lord outshines the depression in our lives. His light will dispel the dark shadows if we open the door to let it in.

Prayer: God, lift our depression with Your light and joy. Help us find the strength to move beyond our darkness.

DON'T GO OVERBOARD

By Karen

*For everything that was written in the past was
written to teach us, so that through the endurance
taught in the Scriptures and the encouragement
they provide we might have hope.*
Romans 15:4 NIV

"Suicidal, defiant, imprisoned, helpless, and hopeless"
are unusual words to describe a character in the Bible.
Yet those very words portray the prophet, Jonah. Jonah
made the foolish mistake of thinking he could escape
God's presence. He sailed in the opposite direction from
where God had commanded him to go. His avoidance
seemed to manifest in despair as he slept soundly in the
ship's hull while a violent storm raged. Upon being
awakened and questioned by the crew, fearing for their
lives, one can almost hear Jonah's sigh as he heard the
crew's solution to calm the waters: to throw him
overboard. Jonah anticipated drowning, but God had
other plans.

Have you ever been so depressed that life became
blurred with feelings of apathy, helplessness, and
hopelessness? Have you ever entertained a similar
solution as Jonah's? Have you tried running away only
to realize there's nowhere to go? Then you and Jonah

have a lot in common!

Depression can take us places we never intended to go and act in ways we never intended to act. We close our minds and turn our thoughts inward to shut out the world. We ignore the reality of our self-centered, self-imposed, immovable position. But God sees it all. He knows it all. And He offers hope.

What saved Jonah? His faith in God's promise to deliver him. God's promises were true then, and they are true now. Jonah was delivered in a remarkable way. His story is one of grace and mercy. And you thought it was all about a big fish!

Prayer: God, deliver me from the pit of despair. May your Word bring hope into my darkness.

If you don't make time for your
wellness, you'll be forced to make time
for your illness.

~ Author unknown ~

Heart of the Matter

1. How does depression manifest itself in you?

2. What are some sources of joy in your life?

3. List some promises of God that can help lift you out
   of times of depression.

Words from His Heart

*He will wipe every tear from their
eyes, and there will be no more death
or sorrow or crying or pain. All these
things are gone forever.*

Revelation 21:4 NLT

What's On Your Heart?

DON'T JUMP!

By Sharon

Don't be afraid, for I am with you. Don't be discouraged, for I am your God. I will strengthen you and help you. I will hold you up with my victorious right hand.
Isaiah 41:10 NLT

I was stressed out and at the end of my rope. A friend offered to put me in a hotel for the night to give me a chance to unwind and relax. That sounded good to me. Coming up the stairs to the third floor, I peered down at the ground below. Reaching my room, I sat on the bed, thinking about the balcony ledge outside.

I picked up my phone. In a state of confusion, I saw derogatory and rejecting texts from friends. The image of the ledge came to the forefront again. I stepped outside. Not only did I feel rejected but also paranoid that someone was coming after me. Contemplating ending it all, something pushed me back into the room. A voice told me to call the police.

Have you ever heard that still small voice or felt a gentle nudge from the Holy Spirit? In those moments of panic and despair, He will uphold you with His righteous right hand. He will speak with reassurance to your heart; He will direct you where you should go. All you have to do is stop and listen. The Holy Spirit provided comfort in my time of need, just at the right time.

God will meet you in the midst of your fear and provide a source of peace in that place. When you are feeling down, He will lift you up. I was slumped over in despair, and He upheld me.

Only later did I realize jumping off the ledge probably would not have resulted in death but rather a severe crippling. God knew and saved me from a perilous plight.

Prayer: Holy Spirit, search me and find those places of fear in me. Open my ears to hear Your calming voice.

A DRINK OF FORGIVENESS

By Karen

*Rise during the night and cry out. Pour out
your hearts like water to the Lord.
Lamentations 2:19a NLT*

Sharon's stress level was higher than usual, but this wasn't the first time I had seen her in such anguish. I downplayed her over-the-top reactions, not fully understanding the dire nature of their cause and effect. Her behavior was unwarranted. Plus, I had no intention of interrupting my evening with my husband to go to a hotel across town for a visit that was sure to be anything but pleasant.

With my mind racing, I cried out to the Lord as I lay in bed wondering, praying, tossing, and turning. *Was Sharon OK?* I didn't learn what had taken place until the next day. Although I didn't want to admit it, the hospital was the safest place for her to be. She had not been prone to delusions before nor had she ever threatened suicide, but this cry for help sounded serious. Truth be known, I was more angry than sympathetic. My prayers, however, soon turned to gratitude and thanksgiving upon learning that Sharon's jumping off a hotel ledge had been halted.

God had watched over her during the night as I had poured out my heart in helplessness, anger, and distress.

God drinks the overflowing, unfiltered "water" from our emotional and confused hearts. Perhaps God had sent an angel to save her.

I cried out again in relief, laying bare my raw contempt mixed with shame that I had expressed so little sympathy. I asked for forgiveness and cleansing. Both were granted.

While we may thirst for answers in desperate situations, we must be willing to fill His cup with the concerns of our hearts. Since He collects our tears in a bottle (Psalm 56:8), why wouldn't He want the "water" from our hearts?

Prayer: Father, cleanse our hearts as we pour our emotions into You.

Suicide doesn't end the chance of life getting worse; it eliminates the possibility of it ever getting any better.

~ Author unknown ~

Heart of the Matter

1. Have you ever felt suicidal? If so, why?

2. Have you ever sensed a gentle nudging from the Holy Spirit? Explain.

3. Are you harboring some unforgiveness in your heart today?

Words from His Heart

*Wisdom and strength belong to God;
counsel and understanding are His.*

Job 12:13 HCSB

What's On Your Heart?

IT TAKES A VILLAGE

By Sharon

Therefore encourage one another and build
each other up, just as in fact you are doing.
I Thessalonians 5:11 NIV

For several years, I drove to the 1920 Club. The Club offers services and life skills management for people with mental health issues. Art and music therapy are some of the programs offered, appealing to one's emotional and expressive creativity. A monthly Bible study provides spiritual enrichment to willing participants. The 1920 Club became one of my primary support systems.

Another source of support is the National Alliance on Mental Illness (NAMI).[8] Their mission is to provide advocacy, education, support, and public awareness for the 1 in 5 individuals diagnosed with a mental illness in the United States. This organization's mission appeals to me. NAMI has become a strong and ongoing support for the mental health community. The program influenced me to become one of their speakers to help champion their cause.

My church has also been an integral part of my support system. From small groups to notes of encouragement to cleaning my home, my church has shown unwavering devotion and support.

Esther enjoyed similar community support through her Jewish community. She received strong family support, especially from her uncle, her religious community, and the entire Jewish nation. She needed as much support as possible to achieve her destiny. God used the masses.

I, too, find that a variety of support systems are beneficial rather than relying on any single source. As my grandmother used to say, "It takes a village."

Prayer: Lord, thank you for the support You provide through others as well as from Yourself.

DIAL "S" FOR SUPPORT

By Karen

Share each other's burdens, and in this
way obey the law of Christ.
Galatians 6:2 NLT

The army of Amalek was doomed to defeat by the Israelites as long as one thing happened: Moses held up the staff of God in his hand. Aaron, Hur, and Moses watched the battle from a nearby hilltop. Moses held up the staff, providing the Israelites an advantage, but the Amalekites gained the upper hand whenever his arms dropped to the ground.

The story in Exodus 17 tells us that Moses' arms became so weary that he could no longer hold them up. Aaron and Hur stepped in to help by finding a rock for Moses to sit on while they stood on each side of him, holding up his hands with the staff. At sunset, the battle was over, and the Israelites claimed victory.

As an advocate or caregiver, have you ever felt you couldn't hold your arms up for another minute? No matter how hard you tried, the weight and intensity of the moment demanded more than you could give. Like Moses, I've had a few moments when I needed immediate and tangible help. Being able to partner with someone during crises to coordinate tasks, make contacts, or provide transportation was invaluable. I learned the crucial role of having a network of secondary support. Communing with God in prayer and releasing my emotional "heap" was healing, but having others share the burden was relieving and refreshing.

The Greek language uses two words to describe "burdens": *baros* are heavy burdens like moving a rock, and *phortion* are everyday burdens like carrying a backpack. *Baros* burdens require assistance; *phortion* burdens do not.

Don't risk losing the battle because you tried to handle the circumstances alone. Get the support you need.

Prayer: Father, send others to help us bear our "baros" burdens when we are overwhelmed.

We can't help everyone, but everyone can help someone.[9]

~ Ronald Reagan ~

Heart of the Matter

1. What are some of your support systems?

2. How has God shown His support for you?

3. Are you carrying any *baros* burdens now? If so, have you shared them with someone?

Words from His Heart

I chirp like a swallow or a crane; I moan like a dove. My eyes grow weak looking upward. Lord, I am oppressed; support me.

Isaiah 38:14 HCSB

What's On Your Heart?

SWEET DREAMS

By Sharon

I will refresh the weary and satisfy the faint.
Jeremiah 31:25 NIV

Refresh the weary; satisfy the faint. These words came from God to the prophet Jeremiah as he slept. His dream was full of promise and hope for the people of Judah. Jeremiah records that his sleep had been "very sweet" before he awoke.

Sleep is not always sweet for a person with mental illness. Sleep can be a source of anxiety and frustration. During times of mania, sleep can be intermittent, filled with racing thoughts and irritability. The instinctive 'fight or flight' response kicks in as the mind perceives a threatening situation requiring one to resist forcibly or to run away.

Depression, on the other hand, has the opposite effect. In a depressive state, sleep becomes excessive, almost suffocating, as it serves as a means of escape. Less life has to be faced when it can be devoted to sleep!

The people of Judah seemed as if they were asleep. Jeremiah had warned them to repent, or else there would be judgment and punishment, but they didn't listen. Exile came . . . for seventy years. Jeremiah's dream gave them renewed hope and motivation.

How often have I responded like the people of Judah by not paying attention to the warnings from friends and loved ones trying to tell me of my wayward actions? Too often, I am afraid. I create an environment of exile, pulling away from what is home to me. But, like the people of Judah, God offers hope for restoration. I may not always find balance in my sleep, but I know God can bring refreshment to my weary body and joy to my sorrowful soul.

Prayer: Lord, give me sweet sleep tonight.

LEAN ON ME

By Karen

Come to Me, all who are weary and
burdened, and I will give you rest.
Matthew 11:28 NIV

We can all relate to being weary and heavy-laden at one time or another. Job stress, family and household responsibilities, childcare and/or eldercare fatigue, deadlines, appointments, extracurricular demands, and commuter challenges can take a toll. Factor in a missing, suicidal, fast-talking, hallucinogenic, mean-spirited, manic-spending, or hazardous-driving loved one, and the stress needle zooms into the red zone.

Relived moments and contrived solutions prevented me from much-needed sleep. Many nights Sharon would call, interrupting the quiet darkness. Consequences had to be enforced. But Jesus doesn't view midnight phone calls as an interruption. He offers words of comfort. He invites us to come into His presence anytime, day or night. His heavenly body needs no refreshment of sleep. The Bible says He neither slumbers nor sleeps (Psalm 121:4). Hallelujah!

Jesus directs His words to the "weary and burdened." How wonderful! We need a shoulder to lean on when we are tired and weighted down. Having someone hold us up lends support during hard times. Being heavy-laden makes us vulnerable to negativity, irritation, and outbursts.

The phrase "I will give you rest" sings like a sweet lullaby to listening ears and exhausted bodies. I visualize a bed with covers turned down and a fluffed pillow. It's almost like Jesus is tucking us in and kissing us goodnight. A sense of contentment washes over me.

Do you feel the power of His words urging you to come to Him? They were spoken by Jesus Himself. They are His promise and His desire to give us rest. We can choose to believe and receive them . . . or not.

Prayer: Father, I am tired and desire to come to You for rest. Show me how to rest in You.

There is a time for many words, and there is also a time for sleep.[10]

~ Homer, The Odyssey ~

Heart of the Matter

1. How is your sleep right now?

2. What disturbs your rest?

3. Do you believe that Jesus can give you rest when you are "weary and heavy-laden"?

Words from His Heart

I lie down and sleep; I wake again because the Lord sustains me.

Psalm 3:5 HCSB

What's On Your Heart?

DELIVERED!

By Sharon

Because of Your name, Yahweh, let me live.
In Your righteousness deliver me from trouble.
Psalm 143:11 HCSB

Mania had taken over my entire being. I wanted help and was convinced that it could not be found in my home state. The psyche ward beds were full in the local hospitals, and I had been turned away one too many times. An alternative was to head to another state, so I drove to the Atlanta airport, thinking I would fly to Virginia to a recovery center I had heard about.

While wandering through a nearby park, I ended up at the Blood and Fire Mission near the airport. As I stood in front of the mission waiting for its doors to open, a black van approached. The back doors of the van opened; a strong, tattooed arm reached out to grab me. Had it not been for a mission patron who pulled me out of harm's way, I may never have been seen again, doomed to a life of human trafficking.

After spending the night at the mission, I walked to the airport. In my lonely and mindless meandering, I came across the airport chapel. Oddly, I heard my name being paged over the intercom. I'd been missing for two days, and my godmother had sought me out. Her voice convinced me to come home.

Twice God saved me! First from the kidnappers, and then from being located by my godmother. My family and friends had been praying for me and my safe return. I was unaware of the intense danger I had been in at the time. God's vigilance, care, and gracious intervention preserved my life and led me out of trouble.

God can preserve your life, too, if you will call upon Him in your time of need. Jehovah Nissi – God is our Deliverer.

Prayer: In the calamities that befall us, O God, rescue and restore us.

ANSWERING THE CALL

By Karen

*Behold, God is my salvation, I will trust
and not be afraid; for the Lord God is my
strength and song, and He has become
my salvation.*
Isaiah 12:2 NASB

All I had to rely on was my trust in God. He alone would give me the strength to withstand the chaos I was in. Two days after Sharon's disappearance, I received a phone call from an employee at the Hartsfield-Jackson Atlanta International Airport. Sharon had found her way to Atlanta, Georgia, but had nowhere to turn after learning that insurance would not cover the cost of her hopeful destination. She was in the midst of a manic episode seeking what she felt would be the help she needed.

I paced back and forth as I clutched the phone, pleading with the airport representative to page Sharon. The frantic tone in my voice was convincing. I silently prayed that Sharon would hear and respond to the page between the pauses and holds. I felt helpless but placed my helplessness into God's capable and trusting hands.

My heart beat wildly with angry love as Sharon answered the page. Despite her renegade spirit, she was glad to hear my voice. She agreed to come home. Only through Him could I rest until Sharon's return – whole and unharmed. I was unaware of how dangerous her situation had been until years later.

Anxiety and fear are natural reactions in the face of crises, but the Scripture tells us that, instead, we can rely on trust and peace as a benefit to our salvation. Strength, joy, and victory come as a bonus.

Today's verse is a song that the Israelites sang upon their exodus from Egypt and their deliverance crossing the Red Sea. This same song will be sung when Christ returns. As believers, we can carry this song of salvation in our hearts.

Prayer: Quiet our anxious hearts and send relief in our time of need. Help us to look to You as our strength and song in the crises we face.

Eventually all pieces fall into place. Until then, laugh at the confusion, live for the moment, and know that everything happens for a reason.[11]

~ Winston Porter Dorey, dealer in furnishings and artwork ~

Heart of the Matter

1. Elaborate on a time when you found yourself in dire circumstances and needed deliverance.

2. How can God be trusted to deliver you?

3. What are some song(s) that give you strength when you are afraid?

Words from His Heart

*Lord, your discipline is good, for it
leads to life and health. You restore
my health and allow me to live!*

Isaiah 38:16 NLT

What's On Your Heart?

CYCLE OF DEFEAT

By Sharon

*But in all these things we overwhelmingly
conquer through him who loved us.
Romans 8:37 NASB*

My educational background is in teaching with an emphasis on Special Education. One of my early jobs was working as an aide to emotionally conflicted students. Once when I was in charge of the class, a student threw a desk across the room. The school administrator did not like my response and requested my resignation. Later on, I taught preschool at a private school. Personal concerns clouded my teaching, causing me to be fired. I then became a certified home health aide. However, an innocent mistake forced me to change companies. While admiring a statue in the foreground of the setting sun of a client's home, I snapped a photo. Thinking I might be strategizing a break-in, I was let go.

Call it what you will – being laid off, getting fired, or receiving your pink slip – losing your job hurts. Job loss can have a significant effect on your emotional well-being. Although not every job I had ended in dismissal, I felt I was in a cycle of defeat. Still, His love sustained me. His provision and plans for me are perfect. Today, despite being on disability, I am blessed with my own condominium, a used car, and sufficient meals.

Joseph was a character in the Bible who also seemed to be caught up in a cycle of defeat (Genesis 37-43). First, he was thrown into a pit by his jealous brothers. Then, he was sold into slavery. Later, he was accused of misconduct with the wife of the captain of Pharoah's guard. Finally, Joseph was thrown into prison but was not defeated. Eventually, Joseph became the second most powerful man in Egypt.

As the Scripture says, we are more than conquerors through Him, even when we feel defeated.

Prayer: Lord, help us look to You to sustain us in our moments of defeat.

WITHOUT FAULT

By Karen

*Now all glory to God, who is able to keep you
from falling away and will bring you with great joy
into his glorious presence without a single fault.
Jude 1:24 NLT*

Can you imagine being born without fully formed arms or legs? I would consider that disabled, wouldn't you? Think again. Vic Vujicic, born without fully formed limbs, earned a college degree with a double major at the age of 21. He also published eight books that have been translated into thirty languages. He has an international ministry called Life Without Limbs and started a motivational speaking company. Incredible! He claims to have an "unstoppable faith" and a "ridiculously good life." And get this – he is married and is a father to four children. Amazing!

Disabled is not a word that has defeated Vic Vujicic. He is quoted as saying: "Put a g-o in front of *disabled*. It spells God is abled." God is always able – disability or no disability.

I believe His ability shows up even more through our disability! That is called "glory." He often uses the most unlikely, the least expected, the direst circumstances, and the oddest of people to manifest His glory. We cannot begin to understand God's ways (Isaiah 55:8), but the wonderful thing is that we don't have to.

Disability was not the word that Sharon or I wanted to accept; however, when Sharon could not maintain a steady job for an extended period, it became apparent that she would need to apply for disability. This was a hard pill to swallow, forcing me to recognize she had a mental disability complicated with social challenges. The truth is, however, that her disability status recognized by the federal government has been a relief, enabling her to receive a stable monthly income. However, we understand God has only ever seen Sharon's ability, not her disability.

Prayer: Father, You can do the impossible. Teach me to accept Your ways.

There is only one thing that makes a dream impossible to achieve; the fear of failure.

~ Author unknown ~

Heart of the Matter

1. When have you felt defeated?

2. What sustains you in your moments of feeling defeated?

3. Do you consider mental illness to be a disability? Why or why not?

Words from His Heart

Therefore, do not throw away your confidence, which has a great reward. For you have need of endurance, so that when you have done the will of God, you may receive what was promised.

Hebrews 10:35-36 NASB

What's On Your Heart?

A LOOK AT LONELINESS

By Sharon

Turn to me and be gracious to me, for
I am lonely and afflicted.
Psalm 25:16 NIV

The week was like a whirlwind. First, a 911 call in the middle of the night sent my roommate to the hospital. Then we learned that her medical condition prohibited her from returning to live with me. The house seemed empty. I was alone. The silence was suffocating. I longed for conversation

Lonely people tend to crave human interaction, but their state of mind makes it hard to connect with other people. My low self-esteem and confidence projected the belief that I was unworthy of attention from others. Research has shown that labeling your feelings can reduce their intensity. Simply putting a name to loneliness can help the brain process the emotion and reduce its impact.

Lonely individuals are scattered throughout the Bible. Hagar is among them. She was an Egyptian servant of Sarah. When Sarah could not conceive, she persuaded her husband Abraham to lay with Hagar, who bore him a son. When Sarah became pregnant years later, she banished Hagar along with her son Ishmael, to the desert. Hagar cried out to God in anguish as she laid her son under a bush to die. God heard her lonely tears of suffering and saved them.

As I face uncertain times without a roommate, I am learning to embrace solitude. God is there to fill the void. He is there to guide me through this transition. And He is helping me find contentment in my solitude.

Overcoming loneliness requires making a change – a change to foster better health and happiness. We must focus on positive thoughts; develop quality relationships; volunteer for community service; and seek people with shared interests and values. Enjoy life!

Prayer: In times of loneliness, let me turn to your waiting arms, Lord.

CONTENTMENT IN SOLITUDE

By Karen

*Yet true godliness with contentment is
itself great wealth.
I Timothy 6:6 NLT*

Some might consider living alone enjoyable, even enviable. You could get to know yourself and your living habits. You may prefer to leave the bed unmade, the dishes unwashed, and the television on all night. Or you may like a quiet environment with everything in its place, the bed made, and the kitchen sink empty.

Sharon's history of intermittent loneliness stems partly from her singleness and her incompatible or non-communicative roommates. Sharon's low activity level is also a contributing factor.

However, she has learned and continues to learn how to combat her loneliness with godliness and contentment.

Jeremiah was a lonely prophet. He had no spouse and no family and was hated by society. Even his profession was despised. Numerous reasons led to Jeremiah's feeling socially isolated. For one thing, his message was to warn the people of Judah – God's people – that judgment was coming. They would have to pay for their sin of idolatry and misdirected worship of other gods if they didn't repent. God could not ignore their sin, but He wanted to give them a chance to change their sinful ways. Still, they refused.

Jeremiah felt the loneliness that came with his assignment. But he found the cure to his loneliness in a dark pit; Sharon found it in the empty room of her condominium; my widowed mother found it after relocating to a new garden home across town. The cure? Contentment in the companionship with the One who knows you better than you know yourself, the One who never leaves your side, the One who knows your every thought. Are you feeling the pangs of loneliness today?

Prayer: Father, be my friend. Fill me with the knowledge of your abiding presence wherever I go.

A pessimist sees the difficulty in every opportunity; an optimist sees hope in every difficulty.[12]

~ Winston Churchill ~

Heart of the Matter

1. What do you do when you feel lonely?

2. What are some changes that a person could make to overcome their loneliness?

3. Differentiate between loneliness and solitude.

Words from His Heart

So be strong and courageous! Do not be afraid and do not panic before them. For the Lord your God will personally go ahead of you. He will neither fail you nor abandon you.

Deuteronomy 31:6 NLT

What's On Your Heart?

PURRFECT LOVE

By Sharon

Whoever has my commands and keeps them is the one who loves me. The one who loves me will be loved by my Father, and I too will love them and show myself to them.
John 14:21 NIV

In my lifetime, I have owned numerous pets. Cats are my favorite. Although finicky and not always cuddly, they express their love and affection in their own way. All of my cats have slept with me (sometimes on my head)! Pax was content curling up on my chest; Hope and Kala Faith were happy sitting in my lap. Selah, my current cat, likes to lie on a cat bed near me on the floor.

One of the adverse effects of bipolar mania is the hurt it inflicts on your loved ones, including your pets. Once, upon admission to the hospital for a manic episode, I left my cat locked in my apartment with no food or water. Karen convinced the landlord to let her in the apartment so she could take care of my cat. Hope was stressed and knew things were not right. Yet, she loved me just the same after I was discharged, greeting me with welcoming purrs.

On another manic spree, I wrongly took Kala Faith with me to Florida to a mental rehabilitation facility. I was forced to board her in an unfamiliar vet office. When I finally returned to pick her up weeks later, she sat in my lap, purring wildly. Her unconditional love warmed my heart.

Jesus Christ demonstrates the same kind of unconditional love my cats have shown to me. His forgiveness is forthcoming. He walks beside me, cries with me, understands my emotions, and feels my heartache. He knows the depth of my despair, the height of my fear, and the breadth of my concerns. His love envelops me with comfort and compassion.

Prayer: Thank you, God, for giving us a glimpse of Your unconditional love through Your small creatures.

PUPPY LOVE

By Karen

Such love has no fear, because perfect love expels all fear. If we are afraid, it is for fear of punishment, and this shows that we have not fully experienced his perfect love.
I John 4:18 NLT

Unconditional love and perfect love are similar but with subtle differences. My dog offers affection without limitations, as defined by unconditional love. His loyalty is evident as he follows me into whichever room of the house I may go. His companionship is a welcome presence and provides protection and greater security when I am alone.

Because of the unconditional love that pets can show to humans, even to total strangers, pets are used as therapeutic facilitators in animal-assisted therapy, better known as pet therapy. The physical, physiological, and emotional benefits of pet therapy are well-documented. Such things as lowering anxiety and depression, increasing social skills, improving interactions with others, motivating a willingness to exercise, and increasing self-esteem are on the list. As a former pet therapist, I know firsthand the difference a pet visit can make.

While my certified therapy dogs have shown unconditional love to many people bringing joy and comfort, they could not erase the fear of many patients in the hospital or rehabilitation. The focal verse today tells us that only perfect love can do that. And that love is found in Jesus Christ.

Perfect love wrapped in human flesh walked this earth over 2,000 years ago. His love has all of the required or desirable elements, qualities, and characteristics. It is complete love – without compromise, without judgment, without punishment.

This perfect love is available to each of us right now. Although the Source of this perfect love no longer physically treads our soil, Jesus sent the Holy Spirit when He ascended into heaven. Jesus had no intention of leaving us alone. He knew we are fearful beings in desperate need of perfect love. Choose to experience His perfect love today.

Prayer: Dear Lord, help me look to You for perfect love to alleviate punishment and fear.

Until one has loved an animal, a part of one's soul remains unawakened.[13]

~ Anatole France, French poet and novelist ~

Heart of the Matter

1. How can a pet provide emotional support?

2. Describe a time when an animal provided a source of comfort for you or someone else?

3. How would you describe unconditional love?

Words from His Heart

The godly care for their animals, but the wicked are always cruel.

Proverbs 12:10 NLT

What's On Your Heart?

HEAD TO TOE

By Sharon

*The human body has many parts, but the
many parts make up one whole body.
So it is with the body of Christ.
I Corinthians 12:12 NLT*

The lady behind the counter said the cost was twenty dollars for each of us. I scrounged around in my pocket for an envelope containing my entertainment fund. Karen whipped out her checkbook, wrote a check, and then promptly recorded it in the register.

Often the person with mental health issues and their mental health advocate do not have the same viewpoint. One area where Karen and I differ is in money management. My money management style involves designated envelopes of cash. Karen reconciles her checkbook down to the last penny. I don't even own a checkbook! She never uses a check card; I use one routinely. Credit cards are essential for Karen. Not for me. I quit using them after learning the hard way that mania and credit cards don't mix.

The scripture for today says that the human body has various parts. Let's consider that money management is associated with the hands. Verse 15 goes on to say that the hand or the foot is no more important than the rest of the body. My hand and Karen's hand function the same but utilize different approaches to accomplish an identical goal.

The apostle Paul is writing in response to divisions within the church created by the people in Corinth. One of those divisions was categorizing spiritual gifts. They considered some gifts to be superior to others. Paul used the body as an analogy to point out the truth.

Hands, feet, and ears (e.g., spiritual gifts, money management) are all part of the body. They work together to make up the whole. And so it is with the body of Christ. Local churches must unify having Christ as the head. God's people, us, with all our differences, are the body.

Prayer: Lord, help me see that my differences are acceptable to You.

THAT'S WHAT YOU THINK!

By Karen

*God works in different ways, but it is the
same God who does the work in all of us.
I Corinthians 12:6 NLT*

"If you take the time to get to know a Bipolar Brain, you may find you are enlightened to a whole new view of the world," said the blog.[14] Medical science confirms that brain structure, chemistry, and function differ from those with and without mental illness. As a "Normal" Brain representative, my eyes have been opened to Sharon's view of the world. Her view is artistic, abstract, and full of color; mine is methodical, organized, and descriptive.

God intends to have diversity in His creation. By doing so, He is exalted through different cultures, tribes, nations, etc. How dull the world would be if we all liked the same things, ate the same food, and wore the same clothes.

Our diversity, however, must function with a unified purpose when it comes to spiritual matters. That is why Paul used the body as a model. We cannot walk without toes or write without fingers. How can we hear without ears or smell without a nose? The body is composed of many parts that work in harmony. Each is important. Competition is absurd. The body needs all of the parts to function as a whole.

Adding to the beauty of God's design is how each body is unique. For example, the "Normal" Brain has a flowing train of thought. A Bipolar Brain has colliding thoughts, like bumper cars. A "Normal" Brain can follow a logical progression, form a plan, and complete it. A Bipolar Brain sees pieces and is deterred by simple distractions. But guess what? God works in different ways. He made both the "Normal" and the Bipolar Brain.

Prayer: Dear God, how wonderful that You created each person differently and that You use different parts to accomplish Your work.

Everybody is different. Everybody has different styles. Just do it the best way you know how.[15]

~ Vince Carter, professional basketball player ~

Heart of the Matter

1. What part of the body would you compare yourself to the most? Why?

2. Identify another example that has many parts to make up the whole.

3. How do you feel God can use your unique abilities in His Kingdom purpose?

Words from His Heart

Everyone should look out not only for his own interests, but also for the interests of others.

Philippians 2:4 HCSB

What's On Your Heart?

WORD UP

By Sharon

My son, pay attention to what I say; turn your ear to my words. Do not let them out of your sight, keep them within your heart; for they are life to those who find them and health to one's whole body.
Proverbs 4:20-22 NIV

Positive affirmations are essential when it comes to self-talk. The internal conversation you have with yourself can be positive or negative. Your personality plays a significant factor in self-talk. If you're an optimist, your self-talk tends to be more hopeful; if you lean towards pessimism, your self-talk tends to be more hostile. One could say that positive self-talk is an indicator of a positive mental health disposition. *I can do this — one step at a time.*

The Bible is full of positive affirmations. Some of my favorites are: I have a spirit of power, love, and a sound mind (II Timothy 1:7); I am crucified with Christ (Galatians 2:20); and I am created with a clean heart (Psalm 51:10). These affirmations encourage my mind, body, and soul.

In the focal verse, King Solomon urges his son to

hide his words in his heart – appearing to be a formula for life and health. Solomon hopes this would give his son positive affirmations upon which to draw throughout his life.

A tangible means of affirmation for me comes from my mentor, Ms. Betsy, who sends me inspiring notes in the mail. Her message refreshes my spirit and brings joy to my heart. Karen also motivates me to continue my daily knee exercises prescribed by my physical therapist. I sometimes send Karen a text telling her I have completed my exercises, and she sends back a congratulatory message. The "atta girl" or "keep up the good work" replays in my head as positive self-talk.

Paying attention and tuning into the words of my mentor, my godmother, and the Bible have helped harvest life and health for me. Find your formula!

Prayer: Lord, let my words be a source of positive and healthy affirmation for others.

WEIGH DOWN

By Karen

At the end of the ten days, Daniel and his three friends looked healthier and better nourished than the young men who had been eating the food assigned by the king. So after that, the attendant fed them only vegetables instead of the food and wine provided for the others.
Daniel 1:15-16 NLT

Self-care, in conjunction with self-talk, contributes to good mental health. The older I get, the harder it is to maintain a healthy body weight. Fried food, pastries, and fruit juices that I once enjoyed are no longer found in my refrigerator. Salads and seafood replace red meat and potatoes. Water replaces iced tea.

Daniel and his three Jewish friends were brought into King Nebuchadnezzar's court to be groomed for the king's royal service. One of the perks was eating the king's food. The meat, however, might have been offered to idols and was certainly not prepared according to kosher guidelines. Daniel refused to defile himself by feasting on the king's food. The result proved advantageous.

Mental health advocates endorse a healthy menu for those with mental health issues. No wonder, since the gut and brain are intimately connected. A poor diet can promote depression and anxiety.[16] Eating fruits, vegetables, nuts, and legumes and limiting processed foods can help reduce symptoms of depression.

A healthier diet instills self-esteem and performance by stimulating more energy, curiosity, creativity, and motivation. A greater sense of flourishing and engagement has been documented.[16]

Increased water intake is a game-changer. Since water makes up 90% of blood, it is vital to keep it replenished. Daniel and his friends understood the value of good water versus wine. Water aids in oxygen transport and skin health; it also promotes faster-working brain power, increased concentration, and improved balance between moods and emotions.

Now you know. It's not just medical advice; it's in the Bible!

Prayer: Creator of life, teach me how to properly care for my body and mind through what I eat and drink.

Loving or hating the life you are living is solely all in your repeated self-talk.[17]

~ Edmond Mbiaka, self-help writer~

Heart of the Matter

1. What are some examples of your positive self-talk?

2. List two Bible verses that bring you encouragement.

3. What are some tactics that you employ for your self-care?

Words from His Heart

Set your mind on things above, not on earthly things.

Colossians 3:2 NIV

What's On Your Heart?

CALLING ON THE LORD

By Sharon

Then you will call, and the Lord will answer;
you will cry for help, and he will say: Here am I.
Isaiah 58:9a NIV

As I lay in bed, I ran the day's activities through my head for the umpteenth time. My stomach was in knots for no particular reason; my head pounded from the overwhelming stress of life. The first thing that popped into my mind was to pick up the phone and call Karen. I believed she would provide the comfort I needed to settle down. Far from my thoughts was the idea of praying or reading the Bible. God did not factor into the solution for my anxiety, although the Bible clearly states that He promises to be near if I call. Did I not trust what the Bible promised?

My thoughts are more controlled now. I meditate on God's promises.

Abraham was the father of many nations. The Bible says that he was righteous because of his faith; but at one point, he feared that he would not have the descendants or the land God had promised to him. God sealed His promise with a covenant to appease Abraham's cries for reassurance (Genesis 15).

Daniel is another person of faith. As a young man, he looked to God for guidance regarding what he should eat and drink when he was brought into the king's court. As he was given more responsibilities, conflict arose. Daniel knew he could call on God to save him when he was thrown into the lion's den (Daniel 6).

If I call my friends when I'm upset, they don't hang up. Their friendly advice provides a momentary source of comfort if they are available. However, true and lasting comfort is found when I turn to God. When I call on God first rather than people, I can always count on Him to be there. My cries for help will be answered as the focal scripture promises.

Prayer: Remind us, dear Lord, in our times of trouble and despair, to turn to You first.

THE MIDNIGHT CRY

By Karen

*The temptations in your life are no different
from what others experience. And God is
faithful. He will not allow the temptation to
be more than you can stand. When you are
tempted, he will show you a way out so that
you can endure.*
I Corinthians 10:13 NLT

I glanced at the clock. It was 2:12 a.m. My husband
answered the phone in a stupor and handed it to me
without speaking. It was Sharon. Again. This time she
just wanted to hear my voice. Last time she asked for
prayer. The time before, I calmed her nerves – all
excuses. Sharon had once again succumbed to the
temptation of her insecurities.

Everybody experiences insecurity from time to
time. It's normal. But when insecurities become a
temptation, God says He will show us a way out so that
we can endure.

A story in Judges 6-8 tells about an Israelite judge
named Gideon. He understood law and authority but had
numerous insecurities, tempting him to deny the truth.
When God chose him to save the Israelites from their
oppressors, he questioned God's decision. He even

questioned if it were God speaking. Gideon tested God by requesting proof of his identity and signs to confirm his decision to use him to rescue the Israelites. God obliged, making Himself known in every instance.

Gideon went on to defeat hordes of Midianites. With only 300 men, they stormed the night with rams' horns, clay jars, and torches. Gideon gained confidence and strength, overcoming his insecurities with God's help.

Sharon finally overcame her midnight insecurities. Instead of picking up the phone, she prayed. In addition, I provided specific guidelines and time boundaries for her to follow. Consequences were applied when she didn't. With patience, time, and practice, Sharon found a way to endure.

Prayer: Almighty Father, praise You for showing us how to overcome temptation. I ask that you be faithful to your Word and show me how to endure the insecurity I am battling.

Friends are lost by calling often and calling seldom.[18]

~ French proverb ~

Heart of the Matter

1. When is the last time you called upon the Lord?

2. Who is someone that brings comfort into your life? What do they do?

3. Take a moment right now to call upon the Lord to meet a specific need in your life.

Words from His Heart

And call upon me in the day of trouble;
I will deliver you, and you shall
glorify me.

Psalm 50:15 ESV

What's On Your Heart?

LIAR, LIAR

By Sharon

So stop telling lies. Let us tell our neighbors
the truth, for we are all parts of the same body.
Ephesians 4:25 NLT

I don't know anyone who likes to be around people who tell lies, do you? Lies take on different shapes and sizes, from omitting details to flat-out falsehoods. There was a time when I used to be so afraid of rejection that I lied. I would hide any action, no matter how small, that I felt might displease Karen or anger her. I even lied about taking out the garbage. I would do anything to avoid unpleasant consequences. Sometimes my lie was one of omission, such as hiding a credit card charge; sometimes my lie was deceptive, such as what I planned to do and with whom I planned to do it.

The Bible tells a story about a woman who lied to satisfy her greed (Judges 16). Her name was Delilah. She used deception to trick Samson into revealing the source of his supernatural strength. Because of his misguided love for Delilah, Samson fell prey to the Philistines when they cut his long hair. He ended up losing his sight and, ultimately, his life. Delilah ended up earning blood money through her betrayal and lies.

I have come to realize that telling lies and hiding

things can hurt people and can cause damage to relationships. Not only do lies foster harm, but they are in opposition to Jesus, who is the Way, the Truth, and the Life (John 14:6).

Deception and lies lead to mistrust. Karen would not reject me, but she could no longer trust me. Speaking the truth may result in consequences, but it is better than hiding behind a bunch of lies. Every step towards valuing truth and resisting falsity draws us closer to God and our neighbors. Planting seeds of truth reaps a harvest of trust.

Prayer: When we are tempted to lie, let us remember it hurts others. Help us to follow the example of Jesus, the Way, the Truth, and the Life.

SEVEN TIMES SEVEN

By Karen

*If your brother or sister sins against you,
rebuke them; and if they repent, forgive them.
Even if they sin against you seven times in a
day and seven times come back to you saying
'I repent,' you must forgive them.
Luke 17:3b-4 NIV*

"It's a lie!"

That's what the Lord told the people of Judah (Jeremiah 7). They thought they were safe and could come to the Temple to worship and then return to their sinful ways and burn incense to false gods. It was a lie for them to think their evil went unnoticed by God. He was angered by their exploits and injustices towards foreigners, widows, and orphans. He was outraged by the idols they brought into the Temple. The people were *not* safe. Their hearts were still wicked when they left the Temple.

How could the foolhardy people of Judah be so bold as to think that God would overlook such wickedness? The foundation of trust built between God and the people of Judah was severed.

No relationship can last without the pillars of trust to support it. Marriages fail and friendships falter. Self-preservation and self-centeredness worm their way into the cracks.

Sharon used lies to protect herself. Some lies were pointless; others were negligent; some were serious, and some were just plain dangerous. All of them were hurtful. They damaged our friendship. They made me mad, but more than anything, they made me sad.

No matter how difficult, lying must stop. No excuses. God offered mercy to the people of Judah if they would repent. He offers forgiveness to us when we choose to deceive, but we, too, must respond with repentance accompanied by sincere regret and remorse.

The word "repent" means to turn 180 degrees and walk in the other direction. Sharon hurt me deeply with her lying. She had to earn my trust again. Her job was to apologize and repent. My job was to forgive.

Prayer: Dear God, give me the willingness to forgive those who have spoken untruths to me.

Telling lies about others is as harmful as hitting them with an axe, wounding them with a sword, or shooting them with a sharp arrow.[19]

~ King Solomon's proverb ~

Heart of the Matter

1. How do you feel when somebody lies to you?

2. What does God have to say about those who lie?

3. Search your heart. Is there someone that comes to your mind you have not been truthful to?

Words from His Heart

Lying lips are an abomination to the Lord, but those who deal faithfully are His delight.

Proverbs 12:22 NASB

What's On Your Heart?

FLEEING TO FLORIDA

By Sharon

*Be strong and courageous, do not be afraid
or in dread of them, for the Lord your God
is the One who is going with you. He will
not desert you or abandon you.
Deuteronomy 31:6 NASB*

Leaving the hospital's psychiatric unit, I knew the discharge was premature. My mind and heart remained unsettled. *How could they leave me on my own?* I decided to take matters into my own hands without the aid of family, friends, or my church. I typed in "mental health facilities in Florida" on my phone and found one to my liking. Setting the GPS, I packed my bags and left in a flash. *Florida, here I come . . .*

With a cat in tow, I drove as far as I could before stopping for the night. I contacted someone back home when my gas tank was empty and the cat's care came into question. My godmother was dumbfounded to learn I was in Florida but was glad to hear I was okay. She told me that my roommate had filed a missing person report.

Even in a manic state, God brought me safely through. Wherever we go, God is with us. He will guide us and provide an escape from our troubles if we seek Him. I felt alone in Florida during those weeks, but God never left my side. In the end, my friends came to meet me and took me back home after my misadventures.

My decision to leave home, especially without telling anyone, was a mistake. But God saw me through the chaos and stood beside me.

When the world seems to turn its back on you, be assured that God will not forsake you. You can remain strong and courageous with the One who goes before you and with you.

Prayer: When we go into unknown places, O Lord, help us remember that You are with us and will never leave us alone.

CASTING OFF BURDENS

By Karen

Give your burdens to the Lord, and he will
take care of you. He will not permit the godly
to slip and fall.
Psalm 55:22 NLT

"Rescued" and "safe" are the words that come to mind when I think of the outcome of my friend's spontaneous escapades to Florida. Determined to do it on her own, Sharon sought help apart from local and state resources, ignoring the obvious drawbacks.

Problems mounted – lots of them. Problems such as parking in a tow zone, medication reactions, identity verification issues, lack of money, boarding and vet care for the cat, unpaid bills, traffic tickets, and communication mishaps from the facility, to name a few. My hands were tied. The best I could hope for was a phone call from Sharon telling me about the day's events, good or bad.

Sharon was in the Lord's hands. He alone would have to care for and watch over her during the six weeks she remained in Florida. I leaned upon the words of the scripture passage, enabling me to still function at work, at home, and at church. This shocking "thing," this wild, unfolding burden, was rocking my world. I found myself casting out new burdens every day.

Who could understand what I was going through? God. Who had the answers to each new problem? God. How would Sharon's cat meet its basic needs during these tumultuous days? God. And, most of all, how would Sharon ever make it home? God. So many questions. Only God had the answers. "He will take care of you," the Bible says. And He did. He took care of me as well as he did for my friend Sharon.

Prayer: Lord, take my burdens, heavy though they may be, and give me a firm foundation.

I think when tragedy occurs, it presents a choice. You can give in to the void, the emptiness that fills your heart, your lungs, constricts your ability to think or even breathe. Or you can try to find meaning.[20]

~ Sheryl Sandberg, COO of Facebook~

Heart of the Matter

1. Describe a time when others felt you needed to be rescued.

2. How has God made Himself known to you when you felt alone?

3. Contrast the difference between "feeling safe" from man's perspective versus God's perspective.

Words from His Heart

I will be your God throughout your lifetime – until your hair is white with age. I made you, and I will care for you. I will carry you along and save you.

Isaiah 46:4 NLT

What's On Your Heart?

DRIVING ME CRAZY

By Sharon

Some trust in chariots and some in horses, but
we trust in the name of the Lord our God.

Psalm 20:7 ESV

I gripped the steering wheel with both hands. Beads of perspiration formed on my brow. The "hands at ten and two" mantra ran through my head. There was nothing out of the ordinary about the day. It was just the way I felt about driving since my automobile accident. Every time I got behind the wheel of the car, flashbacks of squealing breaks and crunching metal consumed my thoughts. Whenever it was possible, I asked my friends to drive so I wouldn't have to.

The accident occurred on a dark night on my way to a Sav-A-Life volunteer meeting. With visibility compromised, I unwisely followed the direction of the driver in the oncoming car, motioning me to turn through a gap in the traffic. His misplaced advice was sorely flawed. The "invisible" car coming from the other direction hit my passenger side, causing me to spin. I panicked and hit the gas instead of the brakes. My car was totaled, and my confidence was shaken.

Driving requires trust in the car and its driver but also in the Lord to get you safely where you want to be. Psalm 20 speaks about the power and victory of leaders and nations, namely King David, and how they must not trust in objects. Instead, they must trust in the strength of the Lord. King David was not shaken because he trusted in the unfailing love of the Most High (Psalm 21:7).

For a long while after the accident, I said a short prayer every time I sat in the driver's seat. Over time, my courage grew, allowing me to feel more at ease (though I will never be fond of driving). Now, I consciously put my trust in the Lord ahead of myself.

Prayer: Lord, help me put my trust in You at all times.

KINDNESS COUNTS

By Karen

Get rid of all bitterness, rage, anger, harsh words, slander, as well as all types of evil behavior. Instead, be kind to each other, tender-hearted, forgiving one another, just as God through Christ has forgiven you.

Ephesians 4:31-32 NLT

I was speechless as I listened to the ER nurse over the phone. Not again. This was Sharon's worst car accident by far. The confusing roundabout debacle was bad enough, but that was nothing more than the inconvenience of finding a second driver to pick up Sharon and her car 150 miles away. This scenario sounded like Sharon's car might be a total loss. At least she wasn't physically injured, unlike the man who suffered whiplash from being hit head-on! How do you overlook a one-way street sign anyway? I could only guess the status of the other three cars involved, including the police car!

My anger and disbelief were mixed with sadness, knowing Sharon was in a manic state. Lashing out was pointless. Sharon's trauma from being handcuffed and shoved to the ground was horrifying. People gathered to witness the scene, recording videos on their phones. A kind, tender, and forgiving heart was what my friend needed.

Mental illness does not often get a reprieve. However, God is eager to offer a reprieve and cancel punishment. The death of His Son, Jesus Christ, on the cross proves that.

The great city of Nineveh is an example of God's kindness and forgiveness. Nineveh's wickedness was rampant. God wanted to warn them of His impending destruction and shine a light into their spiritual darkness. He sent Jonah as a messenger. Although Jonah took some wrong turns along the way, he eventually obeyed the Lord's command. As a result, the city, with its 120,000 residents and animals, was saved.

Kindness, accompanied with forgiveness, goes a long way. Sharon's healing from the traumatic accident and its aftermath depended on it – and so did mine.

Prayer: Dear Lord, plant seeds of kindness in my heart to grow blossoms of forgiveness.

Never drive faster than your guardian angel can fly.

~ Author unknown ~

Heart of the Matter

1. If the driver behind you were to describe your driving habits in traffic, what would they say?

2. Does your driving record need improvement? How?

3. If God were a passenger in your car, would you drive differently?

Words from His Heart

The chariots race recklessly along the streets and rush wildly through the squares. They flash like firelight and move as swiftly as lightning.

Nahum 2:4 NLT

What's On Your Heart?

JUDGE NOT

By Sharon

For in the same way you judge others, you will be judged, and with the measure you use, it will be measured to you.
Matthew 7:2 NIV

Judging and discernment are two different things. You will know if you are judging rather than using discernment by the way that you feel. Do you feel resentful? If you do, then you are judging. Discernment is the feeling of "this is not for me," while judgment is the feeling of "something must be wrong with you."

Mental illness comes with a stigma typically resulting from judgment versus discernment. A staff member at the church I attended was convinced that my behavior would eventually land me in jail. A church member thought my manipulative ways were a tool of Satan. One of my college professors felt my hospitalizations would result in failing her class and lead to withdrawal from school.

My naysayers could have stopped with discernment without passing judgment. Ironically, I did not meet their low expectations. A new church accepted me, and I have never set foot in a jail cell. I passed my class and graduated with a Master's degree in Special Education.

Judging does not mean we cannot identify sin for

what it is. The Bible tells a story about a woman caught in the act of adultery (John 8). She is brought before Jesus expecting to be stoned. Jesus, however, challenges her accusers, saying, "Let any one of you who is without sin be the first to throw a stone." Her accusers begin to walk away one by one until all of them are gone.

As the focal verse says, we will be judged the same way we judge others. Jesus caused her accusers to examine their sins rather than condemn someone else's sins. Not one of us is without fault. Whenever you point an accusing finger at your neighbor, remember that three fingers are pointing back at you.

Prayer: Lord, keep me from pointing fingers at others and ignoring what needs to change in me.

THE JUDGMENT SEAT

By Karen

So why do you condemn another believer?
Why do you look down on another believer?
Remember, we will all stand before the
judgment seat of God.
Romans 14:10 NLT

I could feel my temperature rising as Sharon told me she had received a request not to return to the church she was attending. How could they be so cold? Did they realize how damaging their judgment was? The elders felt as though Sharon was following demonic spirits. *What?* Is that how they labeled mental illness? Sharon's excessive talking and sometimes bizarre behavior took a toll on church members. They wanted her gone.

Jesus admonished the Pharisees in response to their judgment regarding tax collectors. "Healthy people don't need a doctor – sick people do" (Luke 5:31).

Man's judgment can be harsh and insensitive; God's judgment is based on truth. God does not have a different standard for different people. He has one standard for whom no one is exempt. Remember, "we will all stand before the judgment seat."

A story in John 4 illustrates how Jesus withheld judgment from a Samaritan woman who had come to a well to draw water. She was surprised when Jesus asked for a drink because Jews had nothing to do with Samaritans. He identified Himself and offered her living water, despite the five husbands she previously had and the sinful living arrangement she was currently in. He knew everything she had ever done, but His interest was in her eternal life. Love was the missing component.

People tend to avoid people and things they don't understand. With my encouragement, Sharon found another church – one that accepted her but implemented appropriate and necessary boundaries. Once again, love was the missing component.

Prayer: Dear God, people can be so cruel. Even churches at times. Keep me from passing judgment towards those different from me, and help me see them through Your eyes of love.

What mental health needs is more
sunlight, more candor, and more
unashamed conversation.[21]

~ Glenn Close, actress, mental illness
advocate ~

Heart of the Matter

1. Have you been guilty of passing judgment on others recently? If so, how?

2. Jesus was often surrounded by people of questionable character. Who were some of those people?

3. What did Jesus do when He was judged by others?

Words from His Heart

If anyone hears My teachings, and does not keep them, I do not judge him; for I did not come to judge the world, but to save the world.

John 12:47 NASB

What's On Your Heart?

CLEAN ME UP

By Sharon

Woe to you, scribes and Pharisees, hypocrites!
For you cleanse the outside of the cup and dish,
but inside they are full of extortion and self-
indulgence. Blind Pharisee, first cleanse the
inside of the cup and dish, that the outside of
them may be clean also.
Matthew 23:25-28 NKJV

The temptation to satisfy my lust was greater than my shame from watching pornographic material online. I couldn't lay full blame on my dad, although he was the one who introduced me to this world of perversion. Every time I succumbed to the urge, I felt guilty for sinning and also for being the cause of others to sin for my pleasure. I had no desire to be a contributor to the sex- trafficking trade.

Viewing pornographic images contributed to my spiritual and mental health decline. When I closed my eyes, I saw disturbing, yet strangely appealing, images in my mind. I came to the realization that I was addicted. As addictions go, I continued my bad habits. In my heart, however, I didn't want pornography to have control over me. I confessed my addiction to a few close friends and began praying for the compulsive behavior to loosen its hold on me. With encouragement, self-determination, counseling, and strength from the Holy Spirit, I slowly quit. Accountability to others and to God was key.

I remembered how Jesus called out the scribes and Pharisees for appearing good on the outside while selfish desires tainted them from within. He even went so far as to call them "white-washed tombs!" Jesus urged them to cleanse their inner selves before presenting themselves as holy.

David's remorse for his adultery with Bathsheba echoes Jesus' sentiments for cleansing. "Create in me a clean heart, O God; and renew a right spirit within me" (Psalm 51:10).

Jesus makes clear that we cannot be wholly clean without examining the motives in our hearts. Through His sustaining grace, God rescued me from the controlling grip of pornography and cleansed me from within.

Prayer: Lord, deliver me from sin that easily entangles me.

SPIC AND SPAN, MA'AM

By Karen

*Wash yourselves. Cleanse yourselves. Remove
your evil deeds from My sight. Stop doing evil.
Isaiah 1:16 HCSB*

"Cleanliness is next to godliness." That's what my
grandmother used to say. Many think this is a verse from
the Bible, but John Wesley, the co-founder of
Methodism, is the one who penned the phrase.

The practice of cleanliness and godliness began
long before Wesley. Biblical customs in the book of
Leviticus give instructions on such things as what to eat,
how to purify after childbirth, and how to treat
contaminated clothing. Why was this so important?
Because holiness was linked to cleanliness. Old
Testament observances were meant to show sinners how
to be purified from immorality and reunited with God.

Serious skin diseases fall into this category. Leprosy
was viewed as a curse from God and believed to be
connected with sin. However, Jesus debunked the curse,
healing many people with leprosy (Luke 5:13, Matthew
10:8, Luke 17:12-14).

Personal hygiene is something that causes me to
wonder about a person's welfare and journey in life. I do
not envision someone unkempt with oily hair as a CEO,

nor do I see someone wearing a business suit with manicured nails as a trash collector.

One of the stigmas and universal signs of mental illness is bad hygiene. Personal hygiene questions are always asked on disability forms and counseling intakes. *How many times per week do you take a bath/shower? Do you brush your teeth daily?* While mental illness can cause a person to be unable or unaware of the importance of personal hygiene, they are often unaware of the image they project.

As a believer, I desire to appear in such a manner that others think of Christ when they look at me. I worked long and hard to transform Sharon's image of one with a mental illness into one with the love of Christ who happens to have a mental illness. What do others think of when they look at you?

Prayer: Lord, I know You look at the heart, but make me conscious of reflecting You in my outward appearance.

The objective of cleaning is not just to clean, but to feel happiness living within that environment.[22]

~ Marie Kondo, Japanese organizing consultant ~

Heart of the Matter

1. If you were honest, do you admit to having a hidden sin?

2. Have you prayed about hidden sin in your life? If not, consider doing so right now.

3. What are some ways that you can keep your temple cleaner than it is?

Words from His Heart

. . . I plead with you to give your bodies to God because of all he has done for you. Let them be a living and holy sacrifice – the kind he will find acceptable. This is truly the way to worship him.

Romans 12:1 NLT

What's On Your Heart?

LOSING IT

By Sharon

Then he said to them, "Watch out! Be on your guard against all kinds of greed; life does not consist in an abundance of possessions.
Luke 12:15 NIV

Jesus often used parables in His teachings. *Parable* means "to cast alongside." The story is put alongside something else to make the lesson clear. The parable of the pearl of great price (Matthew 13:45-46) describes a merchant who finds a pearl that is so valuable that he sells everything he owns to purchase it. The pearl, symbolizing Jesus Christ and salvation, is worth all the merchant gave up.

The parable of the priceless pearl reminds me of a family jewelry box given to me by my mother. I considered it one of my prized possessions. While in a manic state, I placed it and several other precious mementos in a yard sale. All I cared about was making money to pay off credit card debt. The thought that I would miss the jewelry box never crossed my mind at the time. My greed went so far as to pawn one of my mother's gemstone rings, too. My two class rings sweetened the pot.

I wish I still had all these precious remembrances.

Their monetary gain did not bring me joy. My mental illness robbed me of something important.

Thankfully, those days are behind me, and I am more careful with my possessions. I have learned to avoid yard sales and pawn shops and to treasure all the new keepsakes I have collected. Of course, they don't replace the lost items, but they help ease the pain of the loss.

The truth is nothing I ever possess, regardless of its worth, will be more valuable than the "pearl of great price." The merchant understood this, too. My eternal reassurance, through the saving grace of Jesus Christ, outweighs any earthly mementos and possessions. No one can purchase salvation. It is free just for the asking.

Would you like to own this "pearl of great price"?

Prayer: Lord, I am thankful for my possessions and am sorry for my greed. How truly grateful I am to own the greatest possession of all – salvation.

MERCY ME

By Karen

Seek the Kingdom of God above all else, and
live righteously, and he will give you everything
you need.
Matthew 6:33 NLT

The two small coins hardly made a sound as they dropped into the collection box. How could it? Each coin was only worth a fraction of a penny by today's standards. The widow's offering could not compare to the many wealthy contributors before her.

Jesus watched from nearby and called for his disciples. "This poor widow has given more than all the others," Jesus said. "She, poor as she is, has given everything she had to live on" (Mark 12:43-44 NLT). Others gave only a tiny portion of their surplus. Despite the clanging and heavy thunk in the collection box, it was no substitution for a contrite heart. The widow gave more than all the rest and would likely go hungry that day.

I recall a similar incident early in my friendship with Sharon when I felt immense sadness mixed with confused joy. Sharon had pulled over to speak to a woman on the side of the road. In their conversation, she learned the woman needed undergarments. As it were, Sharon was carrying all of the clothes she owned in the trunk of her car. Even though she was homeless at the time, Sharon gladly gave the woman an assortment of undergarments and prayed with her.

I was so touched by Sharon's act of mercy that I wept. Here I was in my comfortable house, sleeping in my cozy bed while Sharon was staying in a shelter with her car stockpiled full of her personal belongings.

Do we truly recognize the full value of our everyday blessings? Do we put our faith into practice, believing God will supply all we need when we need it?

Prayer: O God, humble my attitude. Open my eyes to see Your goodness so that I may respond accordingly.

We can only be said to be alive in those moments when our hearts are conscious of our treasures.[23]

~ Thornton Wilder, Pulitzer Prize playwright and novelist ~

Heart of the Matter

1. Have you ever lost a prized possession? What was it?

2. The Bible says that "the love of money is the root of all evil" (I Timothy 6:10). Distinguish between "love of money" and "possession of money."

3. How do you personally use your money to express your love for God?

Words from His Heart

God, your God, will restore everything you lost; he'll have compassion on you; he'll come back and pick up the pieces from all the places where you were scattered.

Deuteronomy 30:3 MSG

What's On Your Heart?

QUARRELS AMONG US

By Sharon

*Remind them of these things, and charge them
before God not to quarrel about words, which
does no good, but only ruins the hearers.
II Timothy 2:14 ESV*

Quarreling is seen early on in the Bible in the first book of Genesis. We see strife arise involving Abraham, the patriarch of Christianity. Disputes break out between Abraham and his nephew's herdsmen. The land could not support the sheep, goats, cattle, and tents for both men and their workers, creating overcrowding. Hoping to end the conflict and still maintain good relationships, Abraham decided to separate. Abraham gave his nephew Lot the first choice of land. Lot chose the eastern fertile plains of the Jordan Valley, and Abraham went westward (Genesis 13:5-13).

Verbal fights are words; yet, words can inflict emotional wounds. I remember a quarrel with Karen.

With tears streaming down my face, I flung the paper on the floor. Karen's letter accused me of lying. I picked up the phone to call and beg forgiveness; but before I could begin my plea, she told me she needed some "cool down" time. All I wanted was to hear her say, "I love you," but it wasn't going to happen.

Bipolar rage has a habit of turning things around. A minor incident can balloon into a major fight. It starts with an annoyance and mushrooms into an explosion. My harsh words prompt more harsh words from Karen, and off we go. Depending on the intensity of the argument, a period of hours, days, or maybe weeks passes. While we both feel bad, I am traumatized.

Whether or not you realize it at the time, God hears and knows what words are spoken. Bringing God into the argument reminds us that He hears all. Being willing to listen to the other person in a spirit of love and understanding makes a difference and can result in a faster resolution, knowing God is in the middle.

Prayer: Lord, let us put You in the center of our conflicts to bring about a quicker and more peaceful solution.

UNO ANGER

By Karen

You must all be quick to listen, slow to speak,
and slow to get angry. Human anger does not
produce the righteousness God desires.
James 1:19b-20 NLT

No two people are the same. Each approaches problems with different perspectives. My approach is to find a logical and reasonable solution. Compromise may be involved. On the other hand, Sharon seeks instant gratification with no thought of long-term consequences. Her approach has been known to be irrational and spontaneous.

Sharon has quit a job without having another one, moved out of an apartment with no place to go, and bought a car with no thought of future payments. I did not handle these impulsive actions well. Anger erupted.

God is recorded as getting angry numerous times. He got angry at Moses for using his speech impediment as an excuse not to lead the Israelites out of Egypt (Exodus 4:14). He got angry at the Israelites for making a golden calf (Exodus 32:11), for complaining about not having meat (Numbers 11), and for doubting His promise to lead them into the Promised Land (Numbers 32). I could go on.

Anger is not wrong. How we handle anger is what can be wrong. Sharon used to tell me it was my choice how I responded. As much as that miffed me, she was right.

James gives us a recipe on how to handle anger. The three ingredients are: be quick to listen, be slow to speak, and be slow to anger. If we are honest, most of us do the opposite. We are slow to listen to explanations, quick to voice opinions and disapproval, and quick to strike with anger.

After years of friendship and many disagreements, Sharon and I have learned to remain kind and respectful toward each other using the above three ingredients. "Cool-down" times also help.

The next time your anger does not produce the righteousness God desires, consider enriching your social skills with a game of Uno rather than spewing your hot-tempered vocabulary.

Prayer: Dear God, teach me how to express my anger so as not to damage the relationships of those I love.

Honest disagreement is often a good sign of progress.[24]

~ Mahatma Gandhi ~

Heart of the Matter

1. Give some qualities of what a fair argument would entail.

2. Contrast righteous anger versus uncontrolled anger.

3. What can you do that produces the righteousness of God the next time you get angry?

Words from His Heart

Do not take revenge, my dear friends, but leave room for God's wrath, for it is written; "It is mine to avenge; I will repay," says the Lord.

Romans 12:19 NIV

What's On Your Heart?

FACEBOOK FOLLY

By Sharon

*So whether you eat or drink or whatever you
do, do it all for the glory of God.
I Corinthians 10:31 NIV*

The mysterious writing was incomprehensible. The party came to an abrupt end when King Belshazzar, his wives, nobles, and concubines suddenly saw "the fingers of a human hand writing on the plaster wall of the king's palace" (Daniel 5:5). Daniel was called to interpret the writing of God's hand. And it wasn't good! The Babylonian king was killed that very night and his kingdom was taken over soon thereafter.

My manic writing on Facebook was not exactly comprehensible, either. And it sure wasn't good. My thoughts were scattered and illogical. The responses I received were a collective repetition of questions. *What are you trying to say? Are you OK? You're not making sense.*

Social media had become an outlet for my anger and frustration. I could say almost anything I wanted to at any time. I lost sight of the fact that it was not good to hide behind a screen and spout off words I would never say to someone's face.

The focal verse says that whatever you do, do it all

for God's glory. That includes social media. It would be better for my posts to reflect a positive tone. I can offer prayers for others, praise for what God is doing in my life, expressions of encouragement, and posts of uplifting poems.

Bipolar disorder causes racing thoughts, as my jumbled posts revealed. I was advised to post less and to police my posts to ensure they were appropriate. Not only was my social media content an issue but so was the time I spent trolling and internet surfing. Before I knew it, I had spent two or three hours online.

Is this glorifying to God? What if I chose a more conscious and wiser use of my time and energy? Maybe I could spend less time on Facebook and select more wholesome sites to follow. My time should reflect my love for God.

Prayer: O God, may my social media reflect my love for You and bring glory to Your name.

WEIGHING IN

By Karen

*Do not boast so proudly, or let arrogant words
come out of your mouth, for the Lord is a God
of knowledge, and actions are weighed by him.*
I Samuel 2:3 HCSB

I am from the generation when people dialed a phone to make a telephone call. The phrase "social media" did not exist. Facebook, Twitter, and Pinterest would have been exotic pet names. People from my generation wrote letters and notecards, not texts, emails, and messages. I miss those days when life was simpler. But every generation says that, don't they?

Interactive technologies that share information, ideas, and interests have their place – good and bad. I've discovered that the real heart of the matter comes down to one thing: words. People want to be heard. People want to be noticed, respected, and remembered. Sometimes it's the loudest ones who get the most attention.

Bartimaeus was a loudmouth. His shouting annoyed bystanders, who yelled at him to "be quiet." But the blind beggar only shouted louder as Jesus passed by. "Jesus, Son of David, have mercy on me!" Jesus stopped and requested for Bartimaeus to be brought to Him. "What do you want me to do for you?" Jesus asked.

"My rabbi, I want to see!" Immediately, he could see (Mark 10:46-52).

Jesus noticed and responded to Bartimaeus. He heard his pleas and listened to his emotional request, granting him sight.

When Sharon told me she was going to delete her Facebook account, I was relieved that she had listened to me. Her incoherent posts of arrogance and anger were embarrassing and wreaked of mania. I felt the pangs of her actions somehow reflecting upon me. I wasn't responsible, but Sharon was, manic or not. How would her "actions be weighed by Him?" How would your "actions be weighed by Him"?

Prayer: Dear God, teach me to use my words to encourage others. Make the motives of my actions pure and not proud.

Social media is not a safe space.[25]

~ Tarana Burke, activist ~

Heart of the Matter

1. What are your views on social media?

2. Have you ever used social media inappropriately? If so, how?

3. What do you think Jesus would say if He were to look at your social media posts?

Words from His Heart

Let your conversation be always full of grace, seasoned with salt, so that you may know how to answer everyone.

Colossians 4:6 NIV

What's On Your Heart?

SPEAK NO EVIL

By Sharon

*Likewise, the tongue is a small part of the
body, but it makes great boasts. Consider what
a great forest is set on fire by a small spark.*
James 3:5 NIV

The focal verse compares our tongues to fire. Why fire? We typically think of fire as destructive, burning homes and businesses or harming wildlife. But it can have positive aspects. With fire, we cook food, heat our homes, and make s'mores. Likewise, our speech is destructive and constructive. Our tongues express love, offer encouragement, and praise God. A tongue under control speaks life and truth, blesses and disciplines, and imparts wisdom.

People with ADHD tend to talk more than the average person — way more. We talk because we're excited, nervous, or want to be included in the conversation. Sometimes we talk to fill the silence because silence is hard for us. I tend to talk about myself, which could appear to be self-centered.

If I'm not careful, I can get sucked into a talk tunnel, where I switch topics like a live wire overriding, dismissing, or drowning out another person's conversation. Awkward glances and wary looks get thrown my way. People may write me off as a bad listener or, worse, someone who doesn't care. But I absolutely do care! I want to hear the rest of their stories.

It is imperative for me, as a person with ADHD, to commit my speech to the Lord. No one but God can tame my tongue. James points out that a bit is needed to tame a horse, and a rudder is used to guide a large ship (James 3:3-4). Although the tongue is a small part of the body, it has the capacity to damage relationships and spew hate. We need a guiding Source to speak words of love, peace, and kindness in a world of evil and negativity. God is that Source.

Prayer: Lord, let all I say be committed to You.

DON'T BE A FOOL

By Karen

*But don't just listen to God's word. You must
do what it says. Otherwise, you are only
fooling yourselves.*
James 1:22 NLT

I held the phone away from my ear as Sharon rattled on
and on. I tried to look at her ADHD as a lesson in
patience, but my patience was wearing thin. The
incessant talking impacted Sharon's relationships at
church, work, and school, as well as with the few friends
she had left. My family was also leery of her at
gatherings and holidays. I understood.

A definitive diagnosis of ADHD brought a huge
relief, allowing her to begin treatment. In addition, her
counselor suggested appointing a few individuals to
offer accountability feedback.

With the ADHD under better control, I started to
piece together an underlying issue. Sharon had a
disconnect between listening and heeding advice. This
became an obvious and significant factor when we held
budget meetings. Each week we planned down to the
dollar as to how she should best use her money to meet
all of her expenses. Although tight, we devised a
workable plan; but Sharon didn't always follow it.

Without fully following the plan of action, our meetings had no purpose. As much as I wanted to help, I was fooling myself, and so was Sharon.

God's word is no different. We cannot be on-again, off-again Christians and expect His blessings. What do you think the IRS would do if you paid taxes one year but not the next? As indicated in the focal passage, we should do what God's word says. You can only go so far as to believe what His Word says; but if you don't receive it and validate it by putting His Words into practice, what application do they have? Without application, you are being deprived of God's revealing Himself to you in a real and personal way. Don't be a fool!

Prayer: Dear God, open my ears to hear the teachings of Your word and apply them to my daily living.

Constantly talking isn't necessarily communicating.[26]

~ Charlie Kaufman, American screenwriter ~

Heart of the Matter

1. What are some ways that God can tame your tongue?

2. Whom do you know that talks a lot? How do you best communicate with that person?

3. Compare the communication styles with God of Moses and Joseph, the father of Jesus.

Words from His Heart

Shall a multitude of words go unanswered, and a talkative man be acquitted?

Job 11:2 NASB

What's On Your Heart?

GOOD MEDICINE

By Sharon

*A cheerful heart is good medicine, but a
crushed spirit dries up the bones.
Proverbs 17:22 NIV*

Good medicine is part of my daily routine. I am thankful for my mood-stabilizing medicines. Without them, I would be facing a different lifestyle. Bouts of mania and depression would occur, and side effects of my mental illness would surface. With medication, my bipolar traits are nearly nonexistent. Let me be clear – medicine does not cure my mental illness; it manages the symptoms.

Prescriptions can be a temptation to escape from reality if not taken as directed. In the past, I took too many sleep aids so that I didn't have to face my feelings or circumstances.

Once when I was in a deep depression and took more than prescribed, I found myself delusional – destined for the psychiatric ward.

My friend Luci's overdose of prescription drugs resulted in lung aspiration rather than suicide although she died after two weeks in the hospital. I mourned how playing board games, watching football, and laughing with her would be no more.

Drug misuse is no longer an issue for me. My

transformed attitude keeps me honest with all of my medications. The weekly routine of doling out medicine according to the doctor's orders is followed to the letter as I fill each day of the pillbox.

The writer of Proverbs contrasts a cheerful heart and good medicine with a crushed spirit and dried bones. A cheerful heart energizes the body and prepares it for service; a broken spirit dries up the bone marrow and thins the body.

The difference between my taking prescribed medication and not taking it backs up the scripture. My spirit is energized and ready for service. Medicine is vital in managing my mental illness and its side effects. I would much rather have a cheerful heart than a crushed spirit any day of the week.

Prayer: Lord, You make my heart cheerful. My heart praises the glory of Your healing hands.

TIDYING YOUR TEMPLE

By Karen

*Don't you realize that your body is the temple of
the Holy Spirit, who lives in you and was given to
you by God? You do not belong to yourself, for
God bought you with a high price. So you must
honor God with your body.*
I Corinthians 6:19-20 NLT

Balm for treating sores, figs to cure a boil, mandrakes as
a fertility remedy, garlic for overall health, and hyssop
for cleansing were among the medicinal agents used in
biblical times. Herbs such as aloes, mint, and anise also
demonstrated medicinal benefits. Jesus even used dust as
a medicinal agent to mix with his saliva to place upon the
eyes of a blind man to restore his sight (John 9:1-11).

Although medicine has changed since Jesus' time
on earth, many of today's modern medical practices are
rooted in the traditional forms of Greek and Roman
times.

I used to be proud of the fact that I didn't take any
daily medications. That is a distant memory now after a
cancer diagnosis, a heart attack, and atrial fibrillation.
My symptoms are managed well, for which I am
grateful, but I have had to conform to swallowing a
handful of pills every day. I can't say that I like it, but it

is necessary for me to function at full capacity.

Hallelujah, Sharon is also diligent to take her medications as directed, making her life more manageable and pleasant, not to mention mine and those around her.

Viewing your body as a temple sheds light on how you might otherwise view yourself. We are reminded that our bodies do not belong to us; they belong to God. We are only the housekeeper. It is our responsibility to take good care of its contents. If medicine is required to help in that process, then we should take the medicine God has provided.

Prayer: God, I want to honor You with my body and Your temple by properly taking care of myself.

Don't be ashamed of your medication. It helps you function and live! What's bad about that?

~ Author unknown ~

Heart of the Matter

1. Do you take medications? If so, do you take them as directed?

2. We know that God is the Great Physician. What is your perspective concerning the role of medicine?

3. Physicians must always consider risk versus benefit when prescribing medications. Respond to this statement. How does this affect you?

Words from His Heart

On hearing this, Jesus said, "It is not the healthy who need a doctor, but the sick."

Matthew 9:12 NIV

What's On Your Heart?

OH, WHAT A FEELING!

By Sharon

An angel of the Lord appeared to them,
and the glory of the Lord shone around
them, and they were terrified.
Luke 2:9 NIV

Trust used to be difficult for me, having been hurt many times. Retreating inward, I locked my feelings inside. If I were sad, my face did not show it. If I were excited, my facial expressions did not change.

When I was embraced with an enveloping hug, my body would tense. People described my response as being like a tree. The hurt and rejection I experienced from my past robbed me of the affection needed to reciprocate a loving hug.

Counseling allowed me to accept the possibility of developing loving relationships. Therapy helped me recognize my feelings, taught me about appropriate emotional reactions, and showed me ways to detect others' emotional and behavioral cues.

Karen's and my developing friendship enabled me to trust another person with my feelings. I pushed through the fear of connecting with my emotions, challenging me to build better relationships.

When I think of moments in the Bible where strong

feeling is expressed, I think of the night when angels filled the sky, appearing before shepherds. Of course, the shepherds were terrified. Who wouldn't be? An angel told them, "Fear not, for behold I bring you good tidings of great joy which shall be to all people" (Luke 2:10). The good news was that Jesus, the Messiah, had been born.

The shepherds decided to go to Bethlehem to see this Christ-Child of whom the angels sang. Their fear was turned into great joy. Can you imagine the flood of emotions from witnessing a host of angels and then seeing the newborn Savior of the world?

Over time, I have come face-to-face with my strong emotions, turning from fear and darkness to joy and light. I am now more open to affection and lots of bear hugs!

Prayer: Lord, help me submit my strong feelings to You.

LOVE ACTUALLY

By Karen

We know how much God loves us, and we have put our trust in his love. God is love, and all who live in love live in God, and God lives in them.

1 John 4:16 NLT

Jesus was crucified between two criminals. One scoffed at Jesus, saying, "So you're the Messiah, are you? Prove it by saving yourself – and us, too, while you're at it!" The other criminal defended Jesus saying, "Don't you fear God even when you have been sentenced to die? We deserve to die for our crimes, but this man hasn't done anything wrong." He then directed his words toward Jesus. "Jesus, remember me when you come into your Kingdom" (Luke 23:39-42).

One would expect a mocking response like that of the first criminal. After all, he's a hard-nosed ruffian who has committed crimes punishable by death. But the second criminal shows a drastic change in affect. He exhibits remorse and repentance. Jesus assures him that he will join Him in paradise.

What a turnaround in just a matter of minutes. It happened to a criminal. And it happened to Sharon. Well, not quite like that!

"Affect" refers to the underlying experience of feeling, emotion, or mood. Someone with no affect appears apathetic. Enter Sharon. I was dumbfounded by her lack of affect. I crafted ways to teach her how to respond with appropriate emotions. She didn't know how to express excitement, love, or appreciation. Her body language was stiff, her facial expressions were dull, and her eyes were dark.

How does one break through such a hard outer shell? Only one way: L-O-V-E. Unconditional love. Compassionate, relentless love. That's the kind of love Jesus has for us. Not just for a dying criminal. He offers love to every sinner who will receive it. That's you and me, friend. Partiality is not in the equation when it comes to the love of Jesus. Do you need some of that love today?

Prayer: Reach out, Jesus, and pull me close. Your arms of love can soothe my troubled soul.

Lack of emotion causes lack of progress and lack of motivation.[27]

~ Tony Robbins, American life coach and author ~

Heart of the Matter

1. Tell about a time when you acted differently from how you felt.

2. Does your affect display your true emotions? Explain.

3. Describe the emotional response of these women:

   a. Sarah when she overheard that she would become pregnant (Genesis 18:10-15).

   b. Mary when she was told she was pregnant (Luke 1:26-38).

   c. Hannah when she learned of her pregnancy (I Samuel 1:20-28).

Words from His Heart

*But the goal of our instruction is love
from a pure heart, from a good
conscience, and from a sincere faith.*

I Timothy 1:5 NASB

What's On Your Heart?

HAVE FAITH

By Sharon

For we live by believing and not by seeing.
II Corinthians 5:7 NLT

My mother had a cleaning job with one of the local churches. As an infant, she took me with her and laid me on the altar as she cleaned the sanctuary. In her heart, she dedicated me to the Lord and prayed for His protection and watch over me. At the age of eight, while watching a televangelist, I kneeled in front of the television set and asked Jesus to be my personal Savior.

As I entered junior high, I found myself in a crisis of belief. What is that, you may ask? To understand a crisis of belief, let's look at the disciple Thomas in John 11. Thomas had not been physically present when the other disciples saw and interacted with Jesus following His resurrection, so he experienced a crisis of belief. Thomas doubted whether or not Jesus had risen and was alive. He demanded proof to satisfy his disbelief, which Jesus gladly provided. Proof strengthened his faith.

I, too, felt as if I needed proof to strengthen my faith while at a Christian camp one summer. I was keenly aware of the happiness of others around me as they celebrated their faith, yet I was sad and confused. I asked the camp pastor how I could prove I had faith. He told me that faith didn't make sense and had no logic –all it required was blind belief. I felt a freedom from having to explain my faith.

God has given every person a measure of faith (Romans 12:3). This does not mean you should remain stagnant. On the contrary, growing in faith means getting to know Jesus better, and getting to know Him better means a more abundant life.

Prayer: Lord, give me a blind belief that helps me see You in all circumstances.

A LASTING COVENANT

By Karen

Though you have made me see troubles, many and bitter, you will restore my life again; from the depths of the earth you will again bring me up.
Psalm 71:20 NIV

The word *covenant* is found in legal, social, religious, and theological contexts. A covenant is a chosen relationship between two parties who agree to make a binding promise. Covenants differ from contracts because they are personal and voluntary. Marriage is a covenant. A political treaty is a type of covenant. Covenants usually exist between two equal parties, making it a bilateral agreement; but God's covenants are unilateral. We are the recipients and do not contribute to the agreement other than to accept it, keep it, and receive blessings from it.

Covenants are the backbone of the Bible. The covenant with Abraham plays a central role for believers who are, by faith, the children of Abraham. God promised that Abraham would be the ancestor of many nations with descendants as "numerous as the stars." That covenant still continues today.

A lifelong friendship agreement could be considered a covenant. David and Jonathan pledged their friendship and sealed it with an oath.

One night alone in my bedroom, I made a silent covenant praying to never give up on being an advocate and friend to Sharon Atwood. Despite the turmoil, arguments, accidents, broken promises, lies, and tears, she has the assurance that I will never abandon her. Although my relationship with her has created challenges in my marriage, job, and other friendships, I have kept my covenant.

God's covenant of grace and redemption is available to every individual. We are not required to add anything more to His promise. That is why it is amazing grace! The covenant will not and cannot be withheld because God promised it. There are no contingencies, no unforgivable actions, and no exceptions – only a willingness to pray the Sinner's Prayer. Will you pray that prayer today if you have not already?

The Sinner's Prayer

Dear God, I acknowledge that I am a sinner and am sorry for my sins and the life I have lived. I ask Your forgiveness. I believe Your Son Jesus Christ died on the cross for my sins. The Bible says that if I confess to God and believe in my heart that He raised Jesus from the dead, I shall be saved. I believe this today and accept Jesus as my personal Savior. Amen.

Crazy faith is thoughts and actions that lack reason but trusting fully in what you cannot explicitly prove.[28]

~ Mike Todd, New York Times' best-selling author and pastor ~

Heart of the Matter

1. Do you believe in Jesus Christ as your personal
   Savior? Did you pray the Sinner's Prayer from this
   devotional book?

2. How does faith in Jesus give you an abundant life?

3. What are some benefits of entering into a covenant
   relationship with God?

Words from His Heart

For by grace are ye saved through faith; and that not of yourselves: it is the gift of God.

Ephesians 2:8 KJV

What's On Your Heart?

Scriptures for Living

When you are . . .

Afraid – Deuteronomy 31:8, I Peter 3:14

Angry – James 1:20, Ecclesiastes 7:9

Anxious – Isaiah 35:4, John 14:27

Confused – Psalm 143:8, II Corinthians 10:5

Depressed – Psalm 9:9, John 16:33

Joyful – Psalm 30:11, Philippians 2:2

Lonely – Psalm 25:16-17, Joshua 1:9

Mourning – Matthew 5:4, Revelation 21:4

Physically lost – Luke 15:4-6, Ezekiel 34:16

Regretful – Philippians 3:13-15; Isaiah 43:18-19

Sad – Matthew 10:30-31, Psalm 34:18

Sick – James 5:14-15, Psalm 34:19

Spiritually lost – Luke 19:10, Ephesians 2:1-2

Stressed – Psalm 107:5-7, Luke 12:26-28

Suffering – II Timothy 2:3, I Peter 4:19

Tempted – James 1:12, Hebrews 2:18

Thankful – Ephesians 5:20, I Samuel 12:24

Tired – Jeremiah 31:25, Galatians 6:9

Worried – Matthew 6:27, Luke 12:22-23

Wounded – Jeremiah 30:17, Proverbs 18:14

When you need . . .

Comfort – John 16:33, Isaiah 43:2

Deliverance – Psalms 34:6-7, II Timothy 4:17

Encouragement – Romans 15:5, Isaiah 40:31

Faith – John 11:40, Galatians 2:16

Healing – Jeremiah 17:14, Malachi 4:2

Health – Jeremiah 33:6, Acts 4:9-12

Hope – Romans 5:3-5, I John 3:3

Love – I Corinthians 13:4-8, Matthew 22:36-40

Peace – II Thessalonians 3:16, Exodus 14:14

Reassurance – Psalm 56:3, Isaiah 41:13

Rest – Exodus 33:14, Psalm 23:2-3

Strength – Isaiah 26:3-4, Psalm 59:9

How to . . .

Abide in Him – John 15:4-11, I John 2:6

Be obedient – Hebrews 5:8, Proverbs 15:32

Control your tongue – Proverbs 18:21, Ephesians 4:29

Discipline yourself – I Timothy 4:7-8, Hebrews 12:11

Praise God – Psalm 63: 3-5, I Peter 2:9

Repent – Luke 17: 3-4, Acts 3:19

Seek God – Hebrew 11:6, Exodus 20:8-11

Wait on God – Psalm 37:7-9, Isaiah 39:18

Resources

National Alliance on Mental Illness (NAMI) website is www.nami.org. NAMI HelpLine is 1-800-950-NAMI.
NAMI Connection is a confidential and safe support group for adults living with mental health conditions www.nami.org/connection.

NAMI Family (and Friends) Support Group is a confidential support groups for loved ones of individuals living with mental illness www.nami.org/fsg.

NAMI Peer-to-Peer is an education program focused on mental health, wellness and recovery for anyone experiencing a mental health challenge www.nami.org/p2p.

NAMI Homefront is an education program specifically for loved ones of military service members and veterans who experience symptoms of a mental health condition www.nami.org/homefront.

NAMI FaithNet is an interfaith resource network of NAMI members, friends, clergy and congregations of all faith traditions who wish to encourage faith communities who are welcoming and supportive of persons and families living with mental illness. www.nami.org.

Suicide and Crisis Lifeline, call or text 988. Free and confidential mental health and suicidal crisis line.

www.findtreatment.gov is a confidential resource for persons seeking treatment for mental and substance use disorders.

Suicide Prevention Lifeline is 1-800-273-TALK.

National Institute of Mental Health (NIMH) www.nimh.gov

Substance Abuse and Mental Health Services Administration (SAMHSA) www.samhsa.gov.

American Psychological Association (APA) www.apa.org.

American Psychiatric Association Foundation (APAFDN) www.apafdn.org.

References

[1] Johann Wolfgang von Goethe,
https://www.goodreads.com/author/quotes/285217.Johann_
Wolfgang_von_Goethe?page=3.

[2] Peggy Anderson, *Great Quotes from Great Women*
(Naperville, IL: Simple Truths an imprint of Sourcebooks,
Inc., 2017), 47.

[3] Peggy Anderson, *Great Quotes from Great Women*
(Naperville, IL: Simple Truths an imprint of Sourcebooks,
Inc., 2017), 170.

[4] Napolean Hill,
https://www.bing.com/search?q=quotes+on+strength&form=
MSNSB1&refig=ef6f9607f86d4a01bd55b4078a208024&mk
t=en-us.

[5] Oprah Winfrey, https://www.etonline.com/oprah-winfrey-
reveals-how-she-stays-stress-free-best-time-my-life-
exclusive-88594.

[6] Martin Luther King, Jr.,
https://www.bing.com/images/search?q=quotes%2babout%2
bforgiveness%2bby%2bmartin%2bluther%2bking&id=D3B
8002ED22555E55F9AB86FC49E0462CBB6BCE7&first=1.

[7] Karen Allen, Confronting Cancer with Faith (Birmingham,
AL: Ewe R Blessed Ministries, 2015), 69.

[8] National Alliance on Mental Illness website is www.nami.org.

[9] Ronald Reagan, AZ Quotes, https://www.azquotes.com/quote/241176.

[10] Homer, https://www.goodreads.com/quotes/tag/sleep.

[11] Winston Porter Dorey, https://www.bing.com/search?q=winston+porter+dorey+quotes&form=MSNSB1&refig=203a54802d304fdab038ab734a8e90c1&mkt=en-us.

[12] Winston Churchill, https://www.brainyquote.com/quotes/winston_churchill_156899.

[13] Anatole France, https://www.inspiringquotes.us/author/4009-anatole-france/about-animals#:~:text=All%20ANATOLE%20FRANCE%20Quotes%20about%20%E2%80%9CAnimals%E2%80%9D%20%E2%80%9CUntil%20one,and%20the%20lights%20that%20float%20upon%20the%20waters.

[14] https://themighty.com/2019/05/bipolar-brain-vs-normal-brain.

[15] Vince Carter, AZ Quotes, https://www.azquotes.com/author/2571-Vince_Carter.

[16] Psychosomatic Medicine, 2019 April; 81 (3): 265-280.

[17] Edmond Mbiaka, https://quotesguides.com/positive-self-talk quotes/#:~:text=One%20can%20change%20his%20perspecti ve%20with,us%20on%20an%20almost%20constant%20basi s.&text=One%20can%20change%20his,an%20almost%20co nstant%20basis.&text=change%20his%20perspective%20wi th,us%20on%20an%20almost.

[18] https://www.inspirationalstories.com/proverbs/t/french/.

[19] Proverbs 25:18 NLT.

[20] Peggy Anderson, *Great Quotes from Great Women* (Naperville, IL: Simple Truths an imprint of Sourcebooks, Inc., 2017), 193.

[21] Glenn Close, AZ Quotes, https://www.azquotes.com/author/3004-Glenn_Close/tag/mental-health.

[22] Marie Kondo, https://parenting.firstcry.com/articles/magazine-30-best-cleaning-quotes-and-sayings-to-inspire-you-for-to-take-action/.

[23] Thornton Wilder, quote found in journal of *5 Things I'm Grateful for Today* (Piccadilly Inc.), 2022.

[24] Mahatma Ghandi, https://www.goodreads.com/quotes/809925-honest-disagreement-is-often-a-good-sign-of-progress.

[25] Tarana Burke, https://www.brainyquote.com/topics/social-media-quotes.

[26] Charlie Kaufman, https://quotefancy.com/charlie-kaufman-quotes.

[27] Tony Robbins, https://sourcesofinsight.com/tony-robbins-quotes/.

[28] Mike Todd, https://hips.hearstapps.com/hmg-prod/images/faith-quote1-1593703424.png?resize=480:*.

Vector isolated illustration Vectors by Vecteezy.
Calligraphic ornament. Vintage Decoration.
https://www.vecteezy.com/vector-art/8145698-calligraphic-ornament-vintage-decoration-vector-isolated-illustration.

Some coloring pages provided by Miraj H. through https://fiverr.com.

Meet Sharon and Karen

Sharon Atwood is originally from the small farm town of Hayden, Alabama. As a youngster, she helped PawPaw and MawMaw shell peas, shuck corn, can beans, and make fried peach pies. She left the farm in 1992 to attend junior college before attending Birmingham Southern College, earning a Bachelor's degree in Language Arts Secondary Education. Sharon then went on to complete her Master's degree in Special Education at the University of Alabama at Birmingham in 2001.

Sharon's diverse employment led her to realize she wanted to explore working with the elderly as well as with children, so she became a certified Home Health Aide. While following some of her true passions, she immersed herself in poetry, writing, and artistic expression, offering a welcome distraction from her mental health issues.

As an active member of her local church in Birmingham, Alabama, she enjoys participating in Bible studies. Sharon recently re-entered the workforce to teach reading intervention to elementary-aged children. When she is not writing or working, she likes to cuddle with her cat, Selah. Connect with Sharon through her social media.

Karen O'Kelley Allen enjoyed growing up as the middle daughter of three girls in the small town of Sylacauga, Alabama. Sports and music kept her active on the volleyball court and at the piano and organ bench in local churches. However, her interest in the medical field led her to pursue a Bachelor's Degree in Medical Technology from the University of Southern Mississippi in 1982, followed by a Master's in Education from the University of Alabama at Birmingham.

Karen married her hometown sweetheart, George Parker Allen, and moved to Lake Charles, Louisiana, picking up a mangey dog along the way. After a few years in Cajun Country, they returned to Birmingham, Alabama. Karen enjoys being retired and devoting more time to her writing after working 36 years in laboratory medicine and cancer research.

Karen's bout with cancer in 2003 prompted her to write *Confronting Cancer with Faith*, an award-winning 6-week Bible study of encouragement, comfort, and hope through the trials of cancer (www.confrontingcancerwithfaith.com). She developed Ewe R Blessed Ministries as a result of her writing and international missions work (www.ewerblessed.com) and has a bi-weekly blog (www.ewerblessed.com/blog). Connect with Karen through social media and subscribe to her blog.

Where are we now?

Sharon:

Having found the right combination of medications, I have stabilized my moods, which has kept me out of the hospital for several years now. Perhaps my maturity, age, and continued counseling have also contributed to my improved status. I have found contentment living by myself with my cat. This has proven to be a workable solution financially and socially.

After years of struggling with my mental illness, I finally felt I could tackle a part-time job. I am happy to report that I completed my first year as an elementary reading intervention teacher.

I still struggle with driving issues, anxiety, and large social gatherings, but I have found ways to utilize coping mechanisms to compensate for my needs.

All in all, life is good in my bipolar world.

Karen:

What a relief and joy it has been to experience Sharon's and my friendship without the chaos and trauma from earlier years. Our unique relationship has blossomed into a wonderful blessing.

Sharon has become integrated into my extended family and rarely misses a significant holiday.

As for me, I enjoy the life of a retiree but continue with a part-time job playing the organ for my church. Book clubs, music clubs, lunch dates, community service, and writing groups fill my time when I am not caring for my Mama, my household, or walking my dogs. In addition, I love to travel, whether it be on international mission trips or for pleasure.

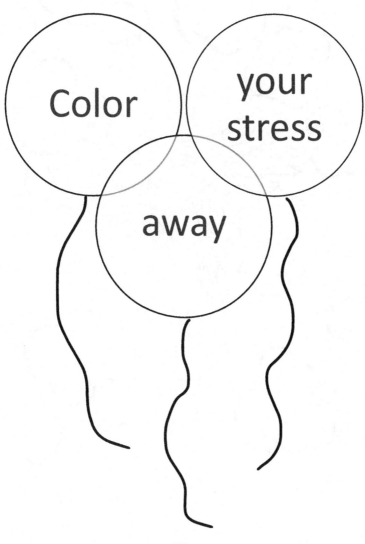

Made in United States
Orlando, FL
02 January 2024

41922612R00183